THE CODE OF "LAOZI"

A Gate for the Great Tao
The Ultimate Principle of Sexuality Hidden in Laozi's Teaching

KAZUKI CHIGA

Translated by
Kiyomi Hirose

CHIRON PUBLICATIONS • ASHEVILLE, NORTH CAROLINA

www.ChironPublications.com

Cover image by Masuko Hamamoto (translator's mother)
Interior and cover design by Danijela Mijailovic
Printed primarily in the United States of America.

ISBN 978-1-63051-916-2 paperback
ISBN 978-1-63051-917-9 hardcover
ISBN 978-1-63051-918-6 electronic
ISBN 978-1-63051-919-3 limited edition paperback

Library of Congress Cataloging-in-Publication Data

Names: Chiga, Kazuki, author. | Hirose, Kiyomi, translator.
Title: The code of "Laozi" : a gate for the great Tao : the ultimate principle of sexuality hidden in Laozi's teaching / Kazuki Chiga ; translated by Kiyomi Hirose.
Other titles: Tao kōdo. English
Description: Asheville, North Carolina : Chiron Publications, 2021. | Summary: "This book is a translation of "The Code of Laozi" ("Tao Code" translated literally), written by Kazuki Chiga, originally published in Japanese by Tokuma Shoten Publishing Co., Ltd. in 2009. He visited an unexplored region attached to a wise man in China, Laozi, had unexpected experiences, and learned the Tao of Laozi. In this book, he tries to convey the Tao beyond the words, with the words based on his experiences. A Japanese Jungian analyst Kiyomi Hirose was called for translating it into English. This book is filled with warmth, love, and mystery of the Tao"-- Provided by publisher.
Identifiers: LCCN 2021010175 (print) | LCCN 2021010176 (ebook) | ISBN 9781630519162 (paperback) | ISBN 9781630519179 (hardcover) | ISBN 9781630519186 (ebook)
Subjects: LCSH: Laozi. Dao de jing. | Sex--Religious aspects--Taoism.
Classification: LCC BL1900.L35 C55713 2021 (print) | LCC BL1900.L35 (ebook) | DDC 299.5/1417--dc23
LC record available at https://lccn.loc.gov/2021010175
LC ebook record available at https://lccn.loc.gov/2021010176

To Predecessors
who made a harmonious world,
and the soul of Laozi

Acknowledgements

First of all, I am deeply grateful to Chiron Publications for bringing this book into the world. It was a long-cherished desire that it could be read, not only by the Japanese, but by everyone, worldwide. My desire bore fruit, thanks to the heartfelt connections of many people, including Kiyomi Hirose, the translator who has devotedly accomplished this very complicated task; Murry Stein, a Jungian analyst who introduced this book to the publisher, Chiron Publications, which accepted this book; Shen Heyong, who wrote the Foreword; and many other people who support me behind the scenes.

I express my gratitude to them all from the depths of my heart.

May the fruit of this endeavor continue creating heartfelt connections, and bring happiness to as many people as possible.

Kazuki Chiga
1 July, 2020

Contents

Foreword

道法自然, 自然本性

Dao, from Nature, and for the Nature

Japanese Jungian analyst Kiyomi Hirose translated *The Code of "Laozi"—A Gate for the Great Tao* by Kazuki Chiga into English. The author had his adventure in the deep mountains of south China, as background and clue, presented his special experiences, and related the unconventional and creative thinking of Laozi.

In recorded history, Laozi (Lao Tzu) was named Li Er, with the word Dan, a native of Kuxian County of Chu State (now Luyi, Henan), and lived between 570–480 B.C.; he passed through Hangu Pass in his later years and spoke five thousand words for the gatekeeper Yinxi, leaving the current book of *"Laozi"* or *"Tao Te Ching."*

The *Tao Te Ching* and Laozi's thoughts are known as the Eastern Sacred Classics. There are thousands of Chinese editions of *Tao Te Ching*, which is a huge body of knowledge; nearly 500 foreign language translations involving more than 30 languages have had far-reaching influence. "Wuwei/No-Action," "Huanghu-Special Trance," "Xuanmiao/Mysticism," "Gushen-God of Valley," "Xuxin-Modesty," "Ziming-Self Enlightening," "Dao following Nature," "Things Must Be Reversed," "Return to Nature"... are all the ideological manifestations of Laozi's "Tao" and "Te."

However, Laozi and his thoughts are not only stored in the books, but also derived from nature, blended with nature, and embodied in the meaning of living and life.

Kazuki Chiga has studied Laozi since he was in high school. He majored in ancient Chinese philosophy at university and liked to travel to China to study. When he traveled to China for the third time, he went to the mountains in southern Yunnan, China, and met the old man, Mr.M, a man with the appearance of a hermit and a lucid power of thinking.

This legendary Mr. M became the origin of *The Code of "Laozi"—A Gate for the Great Tao*. The adventure in the deep mountains, the enlightenment of nature, the experience of life, and the indoctrination of Mr.M, inspired Kazuki Chiga's work, *The Code of "Laozi."* As the author put it: An accidental trip in the deep mountains in China and an unexpected encounter made him finally know with his personal experience what Lao Tzu really said.

From the perspective of Kazuki Chiga and Mr. M cited by him, the essence of Lao Tzu is "Tao"; "Tao" is the natural law followed in the evolution of the universe. The author believes that the village where Mr. M lives evokes the mythical world in human memory. He then touches on "the ancient wisdom which included the sexual energies" in Laozi's work, which is the main message that his book seeks to convey: "the sexual universe."

In the book, *The Code of "Laozi,"* "sex" has multiple meanings, including the experience of sex, the nature of nature, sexual energy, and sacred sex, and he proposes the concept of universal sex. The author believes that all things are born from the ultimate sex/nature, and every cell, molecule, and atom is the product of sex ... and even that sex (sexual energy) be considered as the essence of the universe.

There may be people who find it challenging to agree with Kazuki Chiga's *The Code of "Laozi,"* and may even question the actual existence of Mr. M. However, the expressed thought of the book creates a philosophy of one's own, from a unique point of view.

Originally, the "sex" (xing) of Chinese characters is a pictogram, phono-semantic compounds, and combined ideogram, to convey the symbolic, metaphoric, and analogical meaning.

In its Chinese context, it not only means "sex," "gender," and "procreation," but also includes "essence" and "nature," and the original meaning of life (for instance, in the "Book of Filial Piety," xing is the quality of life. Also, like the "Book of Changes" (Yi): the great virtue of the heaven is procreation; the life of life is Yi; and "the reason why one is born is called xing"—*Xunzi*). "Self-knowledge" (as "The Doctrine of the Mean" says: self-sincere is the nature of xing), and "Destiny" (as "The Doctrine of the Mean: destiny is nature [xing]; accordance with this nature [xing] is called Tao); all of these expressions have the implications of Laozi's Tao.

As far as the "pictogram" and "combined ideogram" of the Chinese character of "xing" (sex/nature) is concerned, it is constructed by the image of the heart and life, implying that the heart seed or the core of life was inherent since birth. The heart seed is the same as benevolence (both the core and the archetype of benevolence contain the image of the heart); it is also the "Yuan," from: Yuan (origination) Heng (prosperity) Li (benignancy) Zhen (perseverance), the four virtues in the "Book of Changes," the vitality of heaven, earth, and universe. Just as the "Book of Changes" says: One yin and one yang are Tao; yin and yang contain the original meaning of Tao; the image of Tao is like Tai Chi, and Tai Chi also contains yin and yang.

Talk about "synchronicity." When Kiyomi Hirose sent me this translation of *The Code of "Laozi"* and asked me to write the foreword, I was heading to the mountains in southern China described in the book, the Miao Villages and Dong Townships, and some ancient villages deep in the mountains that have not yet been opened to outsiders; I took with me *The Code of "Laozi"* and "Luoshu Hetu" (the original images of the I Ching) by A. Cheng.

Here, people are in harmony with nature, innocent and simple. The mountains are high, and the water is long, the air is filled with birdsong and the fragrance of flowers; the old trees become forests, and the "morning glory" really carries the glory of the dawn; the adults are working, farming, and weaving, the children are playing, and dogs and cats accompany each other. As far as my eyes can see, everywhere, it is déjà vu, as if we have met before, smiling at each other, coming from the heart. In the evening, after sunset, the moonlight washes over me while walking in the woods, as if in a dream. Something like a trance of the heart and soul; there was a similar scene described in Kazuki Chiga's *The Code of "Laozi"* ; the harmony in nature and the nature in harmony, this is truly the embodiment of Laozi's thought and the "Tao De Jing."

A. Cheng is a veteran Chinese scholar and artist. Many years ago, when he was investigating in the same mountainous area, he discovered the secrets of ancient Luoshu and Hetu in the embroidery patterns of the Miao nationality. The Hetu and Luoshu are related to the origin of I Ching, the "Book of Changes." The Tao of Lao Tzu is also related to the I Ching. As Tai Shigong said: "I (I Ching) converse in yin and yang"; it also contains Laozi's thoughts.

In 2016, the 20th International Association of Analytical Psychology (IAAP) Conference was held in Kyoto, Japan. The theme of the conference was "Anima Mundi in transition: Cultural, Clinical and Professional Challenges." I gave the plenary presentation with the title: "The Heart of Dao, and the Dao of Anima Mundi," in response to the theme of the conference, focusing on "Tao" and "Trance," and the archetype analysis in Tao, with the background of Psychology of the Heart in Chinese culture.

It is a rare opportunity to be part of the translation by Jungian psychoanalyst Kiyomi Hirose, my Japanese colleague, and to be included in *The Code of "Laozi"—A Gate for the Great Tao* by Kazuki Chiga. The author dedicates this book "To Predecessors who made a harmonious world, and the soul of Laozi." Dao, from Nature, for the Nature, and this is also the preface I would like to present.

Shen Heyong
In Lu Lake, Xixin Island
September, 2020

Introduction

By Kiyomi Hirose

The author visited an unexplored region of China associated with a wise man, Laozi. Then he learned a surprising truth.

The Tao beyond the Tao, a completely different meaning from the well-known Tao, is concealed behind the Tao of Laozi. What is the genuine Tao of Laozi? It is a very profound recognition of sexuality, which is beyond the sexuality we generally know.

In this book, the author tries to convey the Tao which is beyond words, with words based on his own experiences. His hope is that as you read this book, you will feel that something inside of you has washed away, and you will discover the bud of the Tao in yourselves.

THE CODE OF "LAOZI"

A Gate for the Great Tao

The Ultimate Principle of Sexuality
Hidden in Laozi's Teaching

Do you know Laozi,
one of the ancient wise men of China?

If you knew him,
You could hardly believe it
if
the very first chapter of his teachings
was interpreted as follows:

道可道非常道, 名可名非常名。
無名天地之始, 有名萬物之母。
故常無欲以觀其妙, 常有欲以觀其徼。
此兩者, 同出而異名。
同謂之玄, 玄之又玄, 衆妙之門。
(Chapter 1)

"I will tell you about secrets of sexuality.

However,

I would not like to talk about a changeable sexual relationship,

the type you often experience.

Ultimate sexuality is an unnamed essence,

one that has given birth to this universe.

The sexual relationship that you know

is only a pseudo-expression of its true nature.

Thus, we should see the true nature of sexuality

beyond the physical passionate dimension.

Beyond the joy of wild sex you know,

a world of supreme bliss is in its depths.

If you feel an attraction toward merely temporal sexual relationships,

then why don't you try to understand the much deeper world

which is concealed underneath?

This world is the ultimate sexuality, namely,

the sphere of supreme bliss,

something far beyond everything in the universe.

This is what I would like to tell you about—the way to ultimate ecstasy,

namely love."

This is the chapter written as the first chapter of *the book of "Laozi."*
You would be very surprised at this translation because it is completely
different from the one that is well known. But it is not wrong. *The
book of "Laozi"* is a book written in code. The esoteric teachings have
double meanings that have been kept sealed for almost 2,500 years.
Laozi was an Oriental sage and, one of the most famous wise men

known, even to the Western world. However, people have understood his teachings on Tao only in the superficial meanings.

Chapter 1

An encounter with a man, who knew a secret.

—Mr. M, a man with the appearance of a hermit and a lucid power of thinking.

Nowadays, Laozi is known even to Western society as an Oriental sage. But most people have only a superficial understanding of the Tao, the teachings of Laozi. For what purpose did he write his text in code? What kind of secrets did he seal within it?

An encounter that happened completely by chance broadened my understanding. I unexpectedly met a man in a village in the heart of a mountain province in Yunnan, China.

Our encounter had such a great impact on me that it magnified the range of vision in my life by some million times.

I was traveling in China for the third time. As a Japanese college student, I always traveled to China by boat to save money. My attraction to historic Chinese culture led me to choose ancient Chinese Philosophy as my major. On this third trip I finally got the chance to visit the village where I most wanted to go.

I asked a Chinese man to take me to the village, which was isolated from civilization. Because I had met this man on my second visit to China, I knew that he had been to the village once. He agreed. I met him in a town in the south of China, and it took us two days to reach the village deep in the mountains.

The man told me that this mountain range in the south of Yunnan province, an area that also included the northern part of Myanmar, was a kind of Utopia, where more than 20 minority races lived in a very wide space, as large as one half of the main island of Japan, and that the Chinese government had designated it as a place where no foreigners were allowed. I felt anxiety and hesitation, but the man said that all would go well, so I decided to proceed with trust in his words.

We drove a car on an unpaved road through a seemingly never-ending tea field for four or five hours. After that we continued on a very rugged mountain road for several hours until we could go no farther. We slept in the car that night. The next day, we walked from dawn to sunset on a long path where no car could go. At the time, I could not imagine the impressive encounter waiting for me at the end of this long journey.

The narrow path continued at first, and then gradually disappeared. My companion proceeded deeper and deeper into the mountains. All I could do was follow him. I could smell what could only be described as deep nature. My feet felt the rough earth. Within two or three hours, the forest became as thick as a tropical jungle.

Indeed, this area was further south than Okinawa[1] prefecture in Japan, so there were a lot of plants with very big leaves. The climate was one of an everlasting summer, very different from the usual images of China. The leaves seemed oddly huge to me, because I was so used to Japanese nature. I followed the man, imagining that this was what the terrain was like when dinosaurs walked the earth. I elbowed my way through the huge leaves that were touching me, and I felt strangely pleasant, as if I could go back to an ancient era. However, gradually I grew tired.

My guide seemed not to be as tired as I was. Even though it was a pleasant sort of fatigue, it became hard to follow him. No wonder people never walked into this jungle. Maybe we walked for five or six hours. I was so tired that I couldn't think. I was just putting one

---

[1] Okinawa Main Island is located at lat. 26 N. and long. 127 E.

foot in front of the other. Suddenly, a beautiful valley unfolded before me. It was a magnificent valley, with mountains far beyond it. A river spread out as it flowed downward on a splendidly enormous scale. The man finally stopped walking, and we rested as we looked around at the scenery.

This magnificent valley, which unfolded before us suddenly, was not only beautiful, but also something else, I felt. I had only the faintest understanding of nature as beautiful, because I had been so busy throughout my youth. However, this valley taught me about a completely different flow of time. What I felt at first in the depth of this primitive forest was the greatness of time I had forgotten. I felt something boundless that embraced me deeply. Was this sensation a primitive instinct inside me, something brought back to life after several hours walking in deep nature?

I was destined to meet people soon after this, who were embraced by great Mother Nature, and who lived in the forest with the "something boundless" that I felt.

After resting, we walked for maybe another four hours until we reached a village.

The village was located in a very deep remote place that looked like a jungle, and I wondered why it was there. My guide was acquainted with the chief of the village, so we were invited to be guests at the village's biggest house. The next day, my guide returned alone to civilization on the same path we walked in on.

The village, which had almost no visitors from outside, was self-sufficient, and the people had their own culture, one which was isolated from other societies in China. I believe it was probably an ancient Chinese culture that had remained unchanged. Perhaps Mother Mountains or the deep jungle kept people away in order to protect the culture of this village. The inhabitants were all innocent and virtuous.

On the day after my arrival, I met an old man, Mr. M. He was a friend of my host, and he looked like a hermit with his white long beard. His hair was long, too, and tied back in a long, slender rope at his back. The moment I met him, he gave me an impression that was somehow different from anyone else.

His eyes were filled with warmth, and their radiance was bracing when he looked at me.

"Where did you come from?" Mr. M asked me.

"I came from Japan, because I wanted to experience an ancient culture in China," I answered.

After that, he seemed to be interested in me, and he often visited the village chief, with whom I stayed.

He always gave me the impression that he knew something nobody else knew. He seemed to be respected by everybody in the village.

But I never saw him in the evening.

Where could he go apart from the village in such deep mountains? I had no doubt he was a real human being, but I felt as if he was a hero of a mysterious drama.

Several days passed. One day he said to me, as if he had decided something, "Why don't you come to my village?"

What on earth could he mean? Was there another village besides this one?

I answered, "Yes," without knowing what his words meant.

He said, "Come on," and began to walk without turning back and without another word.

Mr. M was 82 years old at that time. But he had the lucid power of thinking of a young man. His back was perfectly straight, too. I followed him, looking at his back and wondering how he kept his youthfulness. Where was he going? I wondered, but all I could do was walk silently behind him.

We walked a long time; longer than I had expected, and we went further into the deep mountains. Birds singing, "kwee, kwee," echoed loudly in the woods. We walked for at least two hours. Finally we reached our destination, I thought, because I saw a small house that looked like a simple temple.

There was a gate, which was similar to, but a little wider than shrine gates in Japan. A sculpture of a bird at the center of the gate was impressive.

We passed through a place like a square yard, which seemed to be at least 50 meters on each side, and Mr. M entered the small, simple, old temple-like house. It looked as if an amateur had built it. I was brought into a small inner room. Mr. M took a book, which was stored carefully there. It was not a typed book, but handwritten, and very old. The word "Laozi" was written on it.

"Laozi" is the name of an ancient Chinese wise man, and also the name of his book. I knew *the book of "Laozi"* very well, because I studied the Chinese version published in Taiwan at university. But this book of "Laozi" was very thin, almost half the size of the one I knew. Looking at it carefully, I noticed that the order of chapters was different from the common book of "Laozi."

Let me explain a little about *the book of "Laozi"* in case you don't know it.

Confucius is famous as a thinker from ancient China, and for the Analects. He had enormous influence on Chinese history. But there was another man in the same era in China who had at least as much influence.

While the ruling classes willingly accepted Confucian teachings, the other man's teachings infiltrated the lower classes. Confucian teachings were about how to lead a life in human society, while the other man searched for a way of life from a framework that transcended human existence. This man was Laozi.

His teachings are called "Tao" nowadays, and are as well-accepted even among intellectual classes in the Western world as Japanese Zen.

His teachings are summarized in this word, "Tao."

He called the way of life which follows the flow of the great universe "Tao."

The word "Tao" was described in ancient China as the way of human beings. But Laozi is known as a person who expanded the word "Tao" from "Tao in human society" to that in the universe.

"When you leave the narrow and organizing minds of human beings, and live by the laws of the great nature, like fish living along the flow of river, you can achieve true happiness."

Such a way of living is known as "the Tao," the teachings of Laozi.

By the way, one reason I decided to write this book was that the interpretation of *the book of "Laozi"* as known worldwide didn't sufficiently relate to "the Tao" of his teachings. I learned this through my relationship with Mr. M, of course. Amazingly, almost no one in China, or even Tao scholars, knew the truth.

Although it may be difficult to believe, "the Tao" of Laozi was in fact a code for a treatise on sexuality.

Laozi is now widely recognized worldwide as an Oriental sage, but most people have only a surface understanding of the true teachings of Laozi. This is because he wrote it in code. Why? And what is concealed?

As you read on, you will learn how I discovered the truth through my own experiences in this remote Chinese village.

Chapter 2

The village of the old man, Mr. M

—A mystical world, where human memory is awakened.

Everybody had very deep insight and powers of observation.
Their sharp observation was completely different from that of
the elderly in civilized society, namely, they read my thoughts
in my every movement, and correctly guessed the experiences
of my past. It was as if they were using telepathy.

I became interested in *the book of "Laozi"* that Mr. M showed me, but on that particular day, he merely asked me about my knowledge of it. That was all.

Was this small temple the village that Mr. M had referred to as his own? Did he say "my village" meaning this temple in a sense of the home of his heart?

Mr. M left the small temple immediately and left me to wonder as I followed.

For about 20 or 30 minutes we walked through a thick forest that looked like a jungle. We met three girls who were playing in a small waterfall. They were around 10 years old. They greeted Mr. M smiling. I noticed that they didn't speak Chinese. They greeted me too, but I just smiled because I didn't understand their language. I was strongly impressed by the young girls.

Two of them wore the handmade clothes of their small ethnic group. Their vivid reddish clothes beautifully contrasted with the green color of trees, as if they were bright birds in the jungle. One of them wore a dress, and looked to be the oldest. She was a child, but her eyes were filled with calm and abundant maternal instinct. She was so very impressive. I felt as though I was embraced warmly in her gentle, unrestrained gaze. As I looked into her eyes, I couldn't help but feel how unfree my own heart was. Another girl had a long cloth around her waist, but the upper half of her body was naked. She had her hair arranged smartly in her own, unique way. I found out later that her name was Mendla. She seemed to be playful and friendly, but at the same time, she had very intellectual eyes. I was attracted by her big, bright eyes, which revealed her intelligence.

The other girl wore a playful skirt made from the leaves of a big tree. Her figure did not appear primitive, but rather stylish to my eyes. Her hair was also arranged elaborately, but differently from the other girl. Some beautiful fresh flowers were tied to her hair. Her figure seemed to blend into the jungle, as if she were an imaginary creature of paradise. Her face was, as were those of the other two girls, extremely good-looking and pure.

I was impressed by their faces more than anything else. Human faces instantly reveal the manner in which they were brought up, I understood. Their playful and innocent eyes were not only cute, but also so pure that they freed me from any restraint. I wondered if I had ever seen such pure eyes before. Their existence pulled me into the illusion that I had strayed into a mythological world.

My interest in *the book of "Laozi"* that Mr. M had showed me, disappeared at this moment. The girls had a much more profound effect on me.

However, this meeting with them was only the beginning of my experiences of this new culture. It proved the existence of a world different from ours.

We left them, and walked for a while; then we came close to a place that seemed to be their village.

So, it turned out that there *was* another village.

The path on which we walked was narrow, but the landscape was broad, with the mountains far behind.

The village was scattered over several houses similar to the Toro Ruins[2] in Japan, but a little bigger. Fields spread out beautifully around them. I felt as though I had traveled back to some ancient time.

The village I had seen previously was, as I had expected, a village that remained just as it might have been in ancient China. But this village had an even more ancient feeling.

I got the impression that the way of their lives was not so different actually from the Yayoi or Jyomon period[3] in Japan.

From the moment I stepped into the village, I was embraced by a marvelous feeling of yearning. It is difficult to express this feeling well, but I might say that it was as if time had stopped and the whole place seemed filled with eternity. It was as if the great memory of the human race beyond my personal memory made me feel that I must have seen this scenery before. I had a feeling of healing and peacefulness beyond description.

I guess the population was less than two hundred. As in the other village, there were neither cars or bicycles. Here, there were no shoes and everyone walked barefoot.

I was strongly impressed with the intelligent faces and beauty of the people in this village. Their presence seemed somehow the opposite of the impression of the village as being so ancient. Their faces were so intelligent that I wondered how people living so deep in the mountains could have them.

Walking a little farther, we arrived at the house of Mr. M. So, he was an inhabitant of this village!

His house was simple but seemed to be the biggest one in this village. His wife greeted me when I entered. She was as beautiful as I expected. When she smiled, her eyes were full of profound mercy. She

---

[2] Toro Ruins is Rice Ruins with pit dwelling houses, located in Shizuoka pref. in central Japan. It dates back to the 1st century, in the late Yayoi period.
[3] From the remote past, about 30 B.C. to A.D. 3

looked younger than 50 years old, and I was very surprised to later learn that she was 73.

Inside the house there were no tatami mats like in Japan, but I felt at home for some reason. Each aspect, such as the smell of the earth in the house, leaves covering the earthen floor and so on, made me feel at home somehow.

I was allowed to stay at the house of Mr. M that night, and I continued to stay there for several more weeks. People in the village accepted my presence willingly even though I was a stranger to them.

The more I got to know them, the more I was attracted by their natural humanity, something we didn't seem to have in civilization. Men were reticent, but they showed their deep thoughtfulness without saying anything. I discovered that, many times, they did something very thoughtful behind my back. The old women tended to talk a lot, so I could observe their thoughtfulness rather easily. I was so impressed by the depth of their insight. Everyone had very deep insight and powers of observation. Their sharp observations were completely different from that of the elderly in civilized society, namely, they read my thoughts in my every movement, and correctly guessed the experiences of my past. It was as if they were using telepathy. Everybody showed a depth of humanity that could only be based on a wealth of experience. I felt as if they were mothers of my psychic home, and that I could entrust myself to them. I felt the power in their hearts that would heal and understand everything. In each family, elderly women were considered the guardian protectors of their families. I wondered if there were a world unknown to civilization that had been created in the psyche of the old women here. If so, I could never understand a verbal explanation, but I might be able to feel it if I lived with them. I intuitively believed this.

Not all uncivilized people have such an attraction. "What could cause such a difference?" This question gradually occupied my thoughts.

They had festivals so often in this village, it was as if they were in a festival mood every day. At one of the festivals I had a very striking experience that answered my question in a very physical manner. I will tell you about it later.

Chapter 3

Secret of Laozi for 2,500 years

—The ancient wisdom, including the sexual energies.

The Tao of Laozi is the code which means sexuality. It is the word which was handed down with the saying that it should remain sealed until the right time came.

Two days after I arrived in the village, Mr. M took me to the small temple again.

Because this village was in the high mountains, it was often foggy. This particular day was foggy. I made my way to the temple with Mr. M along a fantastic mountain path from which nothing could be seen in the mist.

My skin felt chilly in the early morning air. I like such weather somehow. It calms me.

I reached my destination feeling short-winded. The temple was wrapped in the mist. When I entered, I asked him to allow me to take *the book of "Laozi,"* because I was interested in it and wanted to have a better look at it. As I mentioned before, it was almost less than half the size of the present volume, however, I also noticed that there were some chapters that I had never seen before.

Mr. M said,

"More than half the chapters in *the book of "Laozi"* which is known throughout the world, were added later by people who took over the officially-known ideas of Laozi. It is a pity."

I was taught at university that it was clear that *the book of "Laozi"* was not written by only one person, so I was not so surprised to hear this.

Mr. M held *the book of "Laozi"* once again, opened its first page, showed it to me, and asked me, "Do you know the meaning of this part?" His fingers pointed to the first characters. They were:

道可道非常道

This first chapter was the same as the present *book of "Laozi."* I explained to him the meaning I knew, because I remembered what I was taught at the university. These characters meant that "the Tao" was so deep that we couldn't explain it with any words. However, Mr. M said,

"This is how they are understood in the world. However, it is just an external meaning that camouflages the genuine meaning. In fact, the genuine meaning is concealed behind the external meaning."

What he told me later was astonishing.

The book of "Laozi" is in fact a book of esoteric teachings. So, it is said that the genuine meaning is concealed behind an official meaning.

The hidden contents, which Laozi tried to leave to posterity by concealing them, were, in short, the ancient wisdom. Laozi lived 2,500 years ago. However, this timeless wisdom was already lost during his lifetime. He left the secret treasures with the coding technique, hoping that they would be revived in later ages.

Mr. M said that the ancient wisdom was the deep recognition and understanding of the sexuality that all humans had naturally. Modern people associate sexuality only with physical sexual relationships, but sexuality is the source of humanity and the source of the psychic world of human beings. All international actions and thoughts, both good and bad, are created by sexual energies.

Mr. M commented for me on these first words of Laozi in Chinese. Some words were difficult to understand, but he taught them to me one by one. They were as follows:

"All of you are attracted and fascinated by the opposite sex.
There is nothing that is so strong as this desire for the opposite sex.
Sooner or later, you will desire the opposite body.
When your bodies meet, you will experience an intoxication that you have never had before.
Once you experience the zenith of it, you will seek it again and again. It is because you feel it as supreme bliss, even as an extraordinarily supreme bliss for you.
You can forget all of your anxieties even though it is only for a moment. You wander through satisfied love, which is related to everything. You will desire such a condition more and more.
In this way, people catch a glimpse of the world of supreme bliss, to which they unconsciously seek to return."

When I heard the words, "supreme bliss," the faces of the girls at the waterfall came to my mind. I remember that their faces were indeed filled with supreme bliss so that I felt exaltation, as if my heart was set free.

He continued:

"People can go into this world of supreme bliss beyond sexual relationships.
At the very moment they meet the eternal and true, there is supreme bliss.

「常」 means 「不変」 changeless.
Changeless and universal dimensions, that is, absolute dimension which is not influenced by time nor space, Laozi calls 「常」."

As I listened to Mr. M, I could somehow imagine that he had recognition of sexuality that was unknown to me.

We think that sexuality is an instinct which is difficult to control. Because it is such an animal instinct, it is ignoble to talk about it openly; I too have thought this. We are afraid of sexuality as if it were a mysterious monster, and we have to suppress it not to let it out, because we think the sexual desire is something we cannot control. However, the reason why we think like this is because we know our sexuality as nothing more. According to Mr. M, civilized society changed angelic sexuality into evil. So, sexuality is rampaging in our society like a monster as the result of us losing our true nature.

He continued:

"The Tao of Laozi is the code which means sexuality. It is the word which was handed down with the saying that it should remain sealed until the right time came.

「道可道非常道」 means that the Tao 「道」 you know (sexual relationship, sexual ecstasy) is 「非常道」 only the temporal Tao. Laozi tried to allude to an existence of the absolute Tao with this example:

You are caught in a slavish situation in which you have to seek sexual relationships, one after another, or a love relationship that is over only in a moment. Although you are caught by sexual desires, you live searching for love. Although you always seek it somewhere in your psyche, you live caught by time and place, without being satisfied. Thus, you are not free; Laozi indicates so."

I could not understand what Mr. M meant.

"Sexuality is the fundamental power of human beings. The way you deal with it and understand it decides how you live as a human. Its quality and dimension sets your quality and dimension as a human. The way whole societies deal with it has a controlling power to decide the way of the whole society. Until you know 常道 (the eternal Tao), you will suffer."

I could not understand the meaning of his words immediately. However, I knew at once by intuition that a great truth was concealed there.

By the way, why does "the Tao" mean "sexuality"?

Mr. M told me as a matter of course.

I knew later that an important truth was perfectly concealed behind this word.

I will explain it later, but according to Mr. M, "常道 (the eternal Tao)" that Laozi mentioned was the universe itself and consciousness.

In addition, this truth is one that nobody in this world knows, and it is a treasure that was kept secret for 2,500 years, never allowed to be taken out of this home of the ancestors of Mr. M and the other villagers.

I wondered if the origin of the attractiveness of the people in this village had something to do with this secret.

Mr. M said:

"If you visit my village, you will learn to understand what essential sexuality is for a human being."

I wondered how Mr. M, who seemed to be an old man of a minority race, knew the esoteric secrets of Laozi. Who on earth were the people in this village?

Mr. M began to tell me the history of this village as if in answer to my unspoken question.

"This village came into existence with a family. The family lineage took over the old copy and the secret of Laozi. The secret was handed down to the oldest person in the family, from generation to generation. I am a member of the family."

To my surprise, Mr. M was the oldest man in the village!

And, the simple small house which looked like a temple, where I was taken at first, was a festival place where they had worshiped the elder people for many generations.

However, the more I listened to his story, the more questions I had. If Mr. M was not of the Han race, but the eldest man in a minority race, why did he take over the copy and the secret of Laozi?[4]

Mr. M continued:

"It is said that my ancestors were off spring of Laozi, and many things were taken from them."

However, the questions continued to pile up. If he were an offspring of Laozi, then he must be of the Han race.

Mr. M said:

"Laozi was a person who loved the ancient culture. In fact, he didn't create a thought. He earnestly tried to protect the ancient culture as it was, at a time when psychic culture was being lost to civilization. Th erefore, his worldview was not his creation. Its origin is in a Utopia of ancient humans from long ago."

He didn't answer all my questions at this time, but I could perceive that there was a special history in this village connected with Laozi.

---

[4] Laozi is reportedly of the Han race.

Chapter 4

An existent paradise

—People who have exchanges and communicate with the spirits.

They understood that they considered the flowers beautiful because their own souls felt the movements of the flower spirits. The more our hearts are sensitive to beauty, the stronger our sensitivity to the spirits. The spirits guide human beings to higher dimensions, and possess power to make them more beautiful.

I had felt mysteriously relieved since I came to this village, and the relieved feeling took root in me as time passed. I was wrapped in a strange emotion—it was as if I had known this village for several thousand years and had finally returned to my true home.

There might be spiritual memories beyond the physical mind of a human being, and this expansive memory might recall life experiences of thousands or tens of thousands of years ago. This was the only way it all made sense to me. I also had a strong yearning feeling for the people in the village, a yearning I had never felt before. That might be because their natures were stored in my spiritual memory, memories from the Utopia period some hundred thousand years ago.

I was very glad that I could live as the villagers did. I got water from the river and I worked with them in the fields every day. Each activity made me very happy. It seemed that they had good feelings toward me.

The time passed very slowly in the village, and they were not at all oppressed by their labors, such as farming and weaving. While farming, they sang the same song, and they harvested to the singing. Their labors were not as hard as those in Japan. Many crops were harvested easily several months after being planted.

I was strongly impressed by the girls. Although they were Asian, just like Japanese, they looked completely different from the young Japanese women of today, who always appear stiff and strained. Healthy smiling faces, the only thing able to cure a soul. The reticent smiling faces of shy young women. Such smiling faces suited them best. How happy I would be if I could live in this village for the rest of my life!

Fish could be caught at a nearby river. However, because the fishes were messengers of God to the villagers, they ate them only on special occasions. They seemed to be pleased with me. So, they took time to pray, went into the river to fish, and served me the fish to welcome me. It was an enormous welcoming attitude, I think.

Their diets only consisted of natural and simple farm produce. Even if they had poor harvests, they had no trouble finding food because of the blessings of nature: infinite nuts were in the forest, such as acorns and chestnuts. Fruit trees were also planted, and they had enough fruit, including wild fruits.

Women wove whenever they had time. And they took the time to weave elaborate designs even if the cloth was only for practical use. They did it out of their yearning for beauty, not only for necessity in their lives. Their products were all different and all so beautiful. Both men and women wore this bright and vivid cloth. I had only worn mass-produced clothes before, so I learned for the first time how clothes made lovingly by hand enrich the hearts of the people who wear them. Many of the clothes they wove were wrapped around the waist as a skirt. Women often wore them to cover themselves from breast down. Dresses seemed to be used as formal attire. Everybody had long hair that was tied up and arranged elaborately. Both men and women had fresh flowers in their hair. I was impressed to see that they enjoyed personal adornment much more than we do.

As I talked and shared activities with the girls in the village, I came to understand that their concept of beauty is so different from ours.

It became clear later that this concept itself had something to do with the concept of Laozi about sexuality.

When they found beautiful flowers in the forest, they stretched both their hands upward slowly as if scooping up something softly, and turned their hands toward themselves bowing slightly. At first, I thought it might be a spell, but later I learned the reason. They understood that they considered the flowers beautiful because their own souls felt the movements of the flower spirits.

We tend to think that we feel flowers are beautiful because they are beautiful, and that is all. However, why do our souls feel that the color as well as the form is beautiful? It is impossible to explain the theoretical dynamic of our souls theoretically. The villagers perceive the existence of spirits as the cause of sensitivity to beauty, which is impossible to explain as something visible. The more our hearts are sensitive to beauty, the stronger our sensitivity to the spirits. The spirits guide human beings to higher dimensions, and possess power to make them more beautiful.

That is the reason why the girls of the villages strived to exchange and communicate with the spirits, which activated their sense of beauty when their bodies or souls felt something beautiful.

They did so not only toward flowers, but also toward the mountains. I sometimes happened to see them communicating with the mountains in the same way, for example, when a mysterious atmosphere surrounded the faraway mountains, wrapped in the mists.

The reader might wonder why this has anything to do with "sexuality." I would like to continue this book with the idea that I may be able to lead you to having similar para-experiences, just as I did, not based on knowledge but through personal experiences.

The villagers often made wreathes of flowers. I learned later that they were neither for play nor personal adornment, but were meant as signs that they were accepting protection from the spirits. I also came to confront the reality that my lack of knowledge and understanding made me think of their behavior as religious. Gradually I was able to take a humbler attitude, because they perceived a world that we cannot, and they communicated with beings that we do not know.

When I met the village girls at the waterfall for the first time, they were mysterious, like fairies or angels. That might be because the images of their psychic world, which were completely different from ours, were woven into their demeanor. Maybe they actually were with the fairies of flowers. You would agree with me if you saw them.

In fact, their characters were as innocent and soft as flowers. When they felt that their own spiritual brightness had faltered, they tried to reflect on their own hearts and think about what they had done to make that happen. Then they could recover their spiritual power by exchange with the fairies of the innocent flowers. Compared to them, women in civilized societies just buy cosmetics and fashionable clothes to satisfy themselves. Which is the higher beauty? The existence of the women in the village answered the question.

I also later learned that they made their own clothes, not only to pursue beauty, but also as a way of including the spirits of nature in their clothes. They became one with the spirits, and gave life to the clothes by being stirred by the spirits. That was why the clothes they wove shone so brightly.

Some people wore shirts decorated with the leaves of trees, not made of cloth. I have heard that it meant they were protected by the spirits of trees. However, it was also true that they enjoyed their activities. Especially skirts decorated with leaves made them feel playful, and many children made them, too. I was astounded to see how attractive and lively women looked in their natural clothes.

Women also made cosmetic packs of natural substances. I never knew what the effect was, but their skin was beautiful and translucent. Their expressions were also filled with intelligence and decency.

Big, vivid flowers bloomed at the entrance of houses. It gave the impression of the tropics. These flowers also seemed to be an invitation to spirits.

The ground of the whole village was swept by brooms made of bamboo. The faint tracks of the brooms on the ground felt comfortable.

I felt beauty and a strange yearning toward the arrangement of the houses and so on—toward the whole atmosphere of the village.

Men also frequently did cleaning. They did not consider it a chore, but as something that made them feel comfortable. This is a concept that is far different from our own.

Men enjoyed making earthenware, just as women did weaving. It was a form of recreation, art, and religion for them. Their artistic tastes were filled with boldness and strength, ceramic artists in civilized societies could never produce them. The notion was that their activity was a form of spiritual exchange.

In a sense, their entire lives could be called artistic activities. However, their arts were different from ours, and they didn't pursue only mischievous beauty. Their works spoke to my heart as if they were living beings.

They didn't have any electricity, so they went to bed around 7:30 in the evening, and got up around at 4:30 in the morning.

This explanation is in keeping with our concepts of time, but the villagers had no such ideas. They just got up and slept in accord with the movement of the sun. There were no mattresses like futons in Japan. Their beds were made of plants, such as straw covered with a sheet. They had a pleasant scent and were surprisingly comfortable to sleep on.

I laid down looking up at the ceiling in the dim light. The ceiling was not as even as those in Japan, and its structure was bare.

In fact, nothing was even or straight. The pillars were made of natural materials and showed subtle curved lines. By contrast, everything in Japan, such as houses and towns, and so on, were constructed with perfectly straight lines. This space devoid of straight lines gave me tranquility that I had never experienced before. I realized how strongly straight lines influenced the consciousness of human beings. I noticed that nothing was made from straight lines in this village, as there were no straight lines in the realm of nature. Even the roads of the village were constructed using subtle curves. This could be because they were never pressed for time. The richness of sensitivities toward space certainly took priority over the rationality of time in their lives.

Anyway, in this way, my life began in the house as if I was protected by a womb, going to bed and getting up according to the rhythm of the sun.

Mr. M sometimes spent time with me in the twilight. In the glow of the fire in the middle of the house, he told me the myths handed down in the village. His stories were very rhythmical and as beautiful as poems. It seemed these stories were told to the children in each family by the elders.

It was only later that I learned how their houses were centered around the recognition of spirits. When they built a house, they set up a pillar or made a fireplace first, and then performed a ceremony for the spirits to come down into it. After that, they constructed the house around the pillar or fireplace. It seemed that "the house" was a place for the spirits to work, and it deserved the same respect as the womb. So, when their houses were completed, the people prayed for the spirits that worked there. "Human beings, incarnations of the spirits, ask to be allowed to live here." This was their concept of architecture. The houses in this village gave me a mysterious nostalgia, a warm feeling. That might be because they built their houses based on such a concept.

The houses in the village felt brand new. This was because the people who lived in them kept them new out of their respect for the spirits who lived there. The people had a system for renewing certain parts of their homes, usually before the winter and the summer solstices. It was similar to the way our bodies work with old cells constantly being replaced by new ones.

A couple of weeks after I came to this village, I came to understand the language to a certain degree, enough to get by in everyday life.

The word order of the language was exactly the same as Japanese. I knew later that there were only a few languages which have the same grammatical structure as Japanese, including a few of minority races in Tibet and in the southern part of China. Pronunciations of words sometimes change as time passes, however, it is rare that the structure of language changes. In fact, I found later that some of their myths made me imagine that Japanese ancestors had visited them.

Anyway, with the help of the characteristics of the language, I got to understand it rather easily.

Chapter 5

The truth of the deciphered Tao

—What is the Tao?

Laozi applied Shakuji, a kanji character which was borrowed for its pronunciation to transcribe a foreign word, to put double meanings into a piece of poetry. One of the meanings was formal and acceptable, and the other had a meaning that could clearly not be accepted by society at that time if it were written openly.

I live in Japan now. Many years have already passed since I met Mr. M. However, I remember his figure, initiating me into the esoteric teachings of Laozi in the small temple very clearly, as if it had just happened yesterday.

It was a rainy day when Mr. M initiated me into the deciphering of the first chapter of *the book of "Laozi."*

There was no custom of using umbrellas in this village, so it was usual to stay at home on a rainy day. Mr. M invited me to the small temple, saying that it would be rainy in the morning but fine in the evening. We made our way to the small temple in the mist. Mr. M was never wrong about the weather. When we arrived at the small temple, it began to rain little by little as was expected. I liked the sound of raindrops. It made me feel peaceful and at ease.

With the sound of raindrops as background, Mr. M opened *the book of "Laozi,"* and began to tell me the secret of Chapter 1.

The first part of Chapter 1 of *the book of "Laozi"* begins with an antithesis as follows:

道可道非常道，
名可名非常名。

He said,

> "The meaning of this part is interpreted as follows:
>
> The Tao that can be expressed by words
> is not the absolute Tao.
> The Name that can be named is not the absolute Name.
>
> However, this is only the formal meaning, as I told you the other day."

These words at the beginning of *the book of "Laozi"* were interpreted as having this meaning. Of course, Laozi intended to write them so they could be interpreted like this. People had just interpreted them as was calculated, Mr. M explained.

He continued,

> "However, Laozi is saying the following contents at the same time, using a code for the same characters.
>
> The feeling of oneness through the sexual relationship, which can be experienced easily by you, is only a temporal experience. The sexual relationship, known by this name, is only temporal. However, unchanging sexuality has no name to express it."

You readers will be surprised at this interpretation, which is so different from the one most people know. Your surprise mirrors exactly what I experienced with Mr. M.

Some readers will wonder if the sexual relationship is a topic that should be discussed seriously, thinking that it is only one of many human activities. Others will think that Laozi might be a sexual maniac if he sticks to sex so much. In fact, what Laozi was trying to talk about was a world people have not yet recognized. Further, he composed these poems with a double structure, and suggested that something behind sexuality would lead people to "the true Tao" which is understood as the "true way (道; Tao) of life," as the formal meaning in general. "If you understand the double structure and the method to decipher the double meaning of the beginning part of the poems, you would know how to decode the whole *book of "Laozi,"* he said.

Then how do we decipher the secret meanings concealed behind this beginning?

He asked,

"The double meanings are put on an important character in these poems. Do you know what it is?"

I answered,

"Is it the character '道 Tao'?"

He said,

"That is right!"

In the next moment, the key to breaking the seal of the esoteric teachings of Laozi was finally revealed.

He said,

"A key to understanding the true meaning of the Tao is Shakuji."

That was it!

Shakuji means a letter which is replaced with the original letter. It is used only because it has the same sound as the original but a different meaning from it.

Many Shakuji were used in books in China at that time. Laozi applied it with the intent to conceal the esoteric teachings behind the philosophical meanings!

It is said that, not only the beginning, but many sentences are vague and abstract in *the book of "Laozi."* However, now that I know this word "Tao 道" is the letter which is borrowed for another one, such vague and abstract meanings disappear and become restored as completely different and clear meanings. This was the proof that Laozi used this character with the different meanings of the "Tao 道" from the start, Mr. M began to talk.

He said,

"Laozi applied Shakuji to put double meanings into a piece of poetry. One of the meanings was formal and acceptable, and the other had a meaning that could clearly not be accepted by society at that time if it were written openly."

It seemed Laozi tried to tell the whole meaning of his teachings by combining both meanings.

Then, what is the original letter concealed behind the character "Tao 道"?

Is there a single character that changes all of the meanings?

Hearing the sound of raindrops in the small temple, Mr. M began to rub a tablet of Chinese ink into liquid. Was he going to write the character with a writing brush? The sound of his rubbing ink echoed rhythmically in the small temple. He was silent. This silence spread around him and dragged my heart into the boundless depths as was often the case. I was looking at his ink stone imagining that this secret teaching had been kept in this small temple through many generations of his family.

He began to write a character. It was a character that I had never seen. He spoke slowly, pointing to it.

"This is the original character of the 'Tao 擣.'"

I still cannot forget the shock of the next words he spoke.

He said,

"This character Tao 擣 means to 'poke', and it was a secret word which indicated the sexual relationship at that time in China. If you understand the character 'Tao 道' with this meaning, *the book of "Laozi"* will be reborn with completely different meanings from what the worldly believes."

Stillness spread in the small temple for a moment.

What a truth it was! This single coded character had kept the true meaning under seal for 2,500 years!

Mr. M continued explaining.

"He tried to preach the way of human lives.

However, it was not on the same dimension with which the other thinkers preached about at that time.

He knew a way, which was not an ideal thought or a moral order, but connected to the essential human existence.

If you get to know the way, all human suffering will disappear. You will reach the way naturally without hurting anyone or anything.

To tell you about the "way 道" without making mistakes one must talk about sexuality.

Laozi received the revelation from heaven.

Laozi described the Tao doubly like a mirror, namely, the 'Tao 道' which meant the way of human lives and the 'Tao 擣,' which meant the sexual relationship. He figured out how to describe and teach the genuine way correctly without it being noticed that

he was describing the sexual relationship. It is the secret of *the book of 'Laozi.'*
In this way, Laozi expressed double meanings in single sentences. This mysterious book, in which the same sentences were understood in two completely different ways, was born like this."

Why was it necessary to talk about the "sexual relationship" to preach the "Tao 道"? I could not say that I understood it, however, I could understand the reason why Laozi used the word "Tao 道."

Mr. M said, as if he had heard the question in my mind.

"When human beings connect to the universe as one, they reach an absolutely supreme bliss beyond time and space, nothing that compares to the bliss experienced in the physical sexual relationship. It is not different from the stage of being united with all things in the universe, something wise men have described from time immemorial.

What is this feeling of oneness with all things? Laozi tried to convey it using the ecstasy which was experienced in sexual relationships as a hint.

This ecstasy beyond time and space can be experienced without sexual relationships. Besides, it can happen limitless numbers of times. That is what Laozi expressed as "the eternal Tao 常道".

"However, it is not only a hint," he added.

It seemed that the sound of raindrops had become much stronger than before. Mr. M stood up slowly, went to the entrance of the temple and beckoned me. We sat down on the step there together, facing the nature of the mountains in the rain. The air was chilly and a few raindrops hit my skin, blown by the wind. They felt good. It looked like an air shower on a rainy day in the tropics, so the chilly air felt comfortable. This comfort, that my body felt, might also be the comfortable feeling of all living things in this space, such as trees, grasses, and flowers.

Mr. M sat there innocently, as if he enjoyed being one part of this rainy space. My heart also felt a deep, calming comfort. This comfort became gradually deeper in this continuing rainy sound, and brought me into a boundlessly quiet world. As I became conscious of what was happening, I felt that I myself had assimilated in this space in a timeless world. It gave me the mysterious joy of existing in the here and now.

I had never felt this way until I met Mr. M. It happened all the time when I was with him. The space in front of my eyes seemed to be alive. A feeling that I myself was one part of such a world was accompanied with a marvelously happy feeling. No matter what I looked at, I felt like I loved it; this sort of feeling was evoked naturally. Could that be because my heart was influenced by his existence?

Eternal time was always flowing around him. An idea came to my mind suddenly; now I could be happy if a person like him was always close to me. Only by being with him, I felt that my heart took on a quiet rhythm, and led as it should. Only by being with him, something that I could not change myself, was changed. It was as if the psychic world was ordered as well as the space. He gave me the most satisfying answer to the question about the way of human lives and philosophy of life. Moreover, this quiet space itself, that he produced, made me realize the deep meaning of the fact that I was alive.

He spoke in a melodic tone in the quiet space:

"Grasses and trees also enjoy having their bodies and souls washed like this."

His words resounded solemnly in my soul.
This single sentence filled my heart with deep emotion.
His words were just what I was feeling there.
His words continued further.

"By the water given from the heavens, the leaves of trees are washed and revived vividly. The reason why they accept 'the gift' from heaven as it is and enjoy it is because they know the essence of the rhythm of 'time.'"

The stillness spread further when he ended his words.

It felt as if the rhythm of his words resounded, and echoed in the stillness.

After the stillness, he said slowly:

"This world is alive in the rhythm of so-called 'time.' To reach the Tao, you have to relate to the essence of the rhythm of 'time,' and listen to the song of so-called 'space,' just as the leaves of trees enjoy the rhythm of raindrops and also enjoy the rhythm of sunshine."

There was a silence for a moment after his words. I felt as if innumerable silent messages were brought to me with the silence. I got the feeling that I had begun to understand what the essence of the rhythm of "time" was.

After a while, he said as if changing the topic,

"The history of human beings must also be one rhythm."

Mr. M didn't say anything more.

At this moment, the teachings of "Laozi" came to my mind. The meanings of the "Tao" which he was trying to teach people had been kept hidden for 2,500 years. At the same time, sexuality had become a part of the concealed world, with the sacred sexuality of human beings kept under seal, hidden away from the light of the sun. The history of human beings had developed and flourished during this period. However, it seemed that a lot of rather essential things had been forgotten and new forms of unhappiness were behind the prosperity. Does the history of human beings live as a part of a huge rhythm, the way the natural world does? We, the human beings, are in a situation far from harmony, overflowing with different ways of thinking and religion, and countries fight each other over them. Is it possible for us to go along with the huge rhythm of nature, and to proceed to a period where we return to our origin as human beings? In ancient days, human beings, all races, were in a universal world where they recognized God in their sexuality. Going back to our common starting point would be a way for humans to realize harmony in their oneness again, would it not? The most important hint to achieve this might be to relate to the essence of the rhythm of "time."

Such ideas flashed across my mind.

Mr. M said nothing. It was as if he were letting me think.

I sometimes experienced such situations. When I was with him, I had thoughts I had never had before. They entered my mind, one by one, during the silence.

We came back again to the small temple from the world beyond time and space. I felt that the same temple was in a completely different dimension from a little while ago.

He opened *the book of "Laozi"* once more.

The whole of Chapter 1 was written as follows.

道可道非常道, (1) [5]
名可名非常名。(2)
無名天地之始, (3)
有名萬物之母。(4)
故常無欲以觀其妙, (5)
常有欲以觀其徼。(6)
此兩者, 同出而異名。(7)
同謂之, 玄玄之又玄, 衆妙之門。(8)

Mr. M explained the meaning of this part as follows:

---

[5] Translator added numbers to each line to help readers find the references and meanings later.

"The "Tao" you often perform, and mention,
is only the trivial Tao.
I tell you the eternal and ultimate Tao now.
That, which produced this universe,
was the ultimate Tao that had no name.
The Tao you know is only a pseudo-phenomenon.
Therefore, we have to be separated from the greedy
dimension, and see the genuine essence of the Tao.
Even though there is an exquisite world of supreme bliss
behind it,
if people think of the Tao only as a target of sexual desires,
they will remain bound to the rough world,
which they themselves describe.
The Tao you know is only the temporal expression of the
Tao,
in which you cannot see its origin.
You are even attracted mysteriously by this physical Tao,
however, why don't you try to understand the world behind
it, which is many more times profound?
It is the very ultimate Tao,
namely, the sphere of supreme bliss
beyond everything in the universe."

When I listened to his explanations, I felt as though I was seeing a huge universe in a few verses. I felt that these few words contained the answers that would solve all of the problems of human beings, and I was driven by an impulse to thoroughly study the depth of these words, as I was being taught the secret of the code. I came to wonder whether the answer to the question of the essence of the rhythm of "time" that he mentioned was also under seal in those words, so I was driven by an impulse to ask him about it directly.

However, it might have been transmitted by him to me silently, beyond words.

Now, I come back to the interpretation.

The formal meaning of this first chapter, which is well known in general, is as follows.

The Tao that can be expressed by words
is not the absolute Tao. (1)
The Name that can be named
is not the absolute Name. (2)
However, each existence,
was born from the named existence (4)
that was created from the nameless movements. (3)
Therefore, when you become free of avarice,
you come to see the mysterious movements. (5)
You see only the superficial world opposing it
as long as you have avarice. (6)
Both the named sphere and the nameless sphere
come from the same source,
with the difference named or nameless. (7)
The deepest movements behind these very profound
movements create everything. (8)

As you see, this chapter is taught as a completely abstract idea, a completely superficial symbolic philosophy.

If I add my own interpretation to this chapter on the basis of Mr. M's explanation, it would be as follows.

First of all, it is not natural that the following parts "故常無欲以觀其妙" (5) and "常有欲以觀其徼" (6) suddenly jump to the topic of desire in its external meanings. In reality some of the translators of *the book of "Laozi"* ignore this part completely to avoid making the meanings unnatural.

However, if you interpret the "Tao 道" in the meaning I mentioned before, the meanings of all parts are connected in a natural flow. This is the evidence that Laozi thought out the secret meaning of the "Tao 道" first, and then took it into consideration so that it could be interpreted also as was generally understood.

The connection between the first lines, "道可道非常道" (1) and "名可名非常名" (2), and the following lines, "無名天地之始" (3) and "有名萬物之母" (4), is also unnatural in the general interpretation. "無名 nameless" here shows clearly "道 the Tao" that Laozi wanted to teach, according to the flow of the sentences. However, "道 the Tao" of Laozi in the general meaning should indicate "the way of essential and natural life of a human being." We can only interpret this part intuitively, saying "the natural, artless way of life is what created heaven and earth."

In addition, in the superficial meaning, a contradiction arises. Namely, when Laozi said "道可道非常道" (1) (the Tao that can be expressed in words is not the absolute Tao), he meant that the Tao could not be discussed in words, but then he talked about the Tao in *the book of "Laozi."* However, when you know the secret meaning, it becomes clear that this poem doesn't talk about merely abstract theory.

The device of putting double meanings in *the book of "Laozi"* is already evident in these beginning words.

It is not easy to interpret "道可道非常道" (1). The genuine meaning can be understood only when you try to understand it combined with the following sentence, "名可名非常名" (2). This is a typical tendency of text written by Laozi, and almost all parts of *the book of "Laozi"* are composed by such antitheses. Mr. M said that it had a kind of rhythm, and the rhythm running in *the book of "Laozi"* showed a feature of human beings grasping the rhythm of the universe. However, I would like to try to interpret it here as a thinking pattern of Laozi.

If you know the thinking pattern of Laozi in which he understands Yin and Yang as a couple, then within his written expressions, you can easily imagine how he came upon the idea of expressing his teachings by combining both meanings of the character "道 Tao" as a Shakuji and its original character "擣 Tao."

Laozi conveys a concept by the relative Yin and Yang, in which he repeats an antithesis coded by a Shakuji in the expression of poetic antithesis. Compared to prose, poems can convey a lot of information in a few letters. However, in *the book of "Laozi,"* only a few words convey infinite visions and bring forth infinite information based on the inexhaustible spring of poems coded beyond even such poetic expression. According to Mr. M, it seems that this expression technique of Laozi itself, which fulfills his original symbolic universe beyond not only prose but also poetic expressions, shows the rules of the universe.

The book of "Laozi" written as I mentioned above is conveying one meaning. Of course, both of the meanings are present, namely the secret meanings in code and the external ones.

Therefore, it is nonsense to translate *the book of "Laozi"* literally. If I interpret the first chapter with this complete viewpoint, the meanings are as follows:

> The Tao which can be described in words as the true Tao,
> is not the unchangeable absolute truth at all.
> Something truly unchangeable
> cannot be understood within these words.
> However, there is a moment when anybody can catch a glimpse of the true Tao.
> It is a sexual sensation through the body,
> positioned in the opposite to the tip of the head.
> However, it is also only a model of the true Tao.
> The Tao you know (sexual relationship and the ecstasy following it)
> is only an imitative expression of the true Tao.
> The unchangeable activity of the universe
> concealed in the far depths of it is the true Tao.
> Therefore, you see, the essence of this universe
> is the ultimate ecstasy.

When you know the way his teachings are written, you understand that the words other than "道 the Tao" in *the book of "Laozi"* also have another meaning which is concealed in the poems.

For example, Chapter 21 is written as follows.

孔德之容, 惟道是從。
道之爲物, 惟恍惟惚。
惚兮恍兮, 其中有象。
恍兮惚兮, 其中有物。
窈兮冥兮, 其中有精。

I will explain the first line "孔德之容,惟道是從。" later. Even readers who are not used to reading Chinese compositions imagine that ejaculation occurs when a man is in ecstasy,[6] which is described in the second to fifth lines. One meaning is described by the antithesis in the third to fifth line. On the other hand, "惟恍惟惚" is understood with the meaning of "vagueness" as the external meaning. There are many parts in *the book of "Laozi"* like this, where they are composed in order to be understood in a double way.

These words of Laozi "大道廢, 有仁義。" (Chapter 18) are well known. These famous words without any sexual expressions can also bring the deeper interpretation, according to the twofold structures.

The known meaning of these words is as follows.

When the essential ways of human beings were lost, humanity and justice (such as discipline, morals, ethics and so on) which people in the world valued became necessary. (Therefore, they don't bring true happiness to people.)

However, Laozi concealed the deeper meanings behind it. "大道 (the great Tao literally)" in this part also means the great Tao, as it were, universal sexuality, namely, "the sacred nature in the great universe."

This part is also composed by an antithesis in the actual *book of "Laozi."*

---

[6] ecstasy=惟恍惟惚. Even if you cannot read Chinese, if you can understand at least the meaning of each Chinese letter like Japanese letters, you can guess the meaning of Chinese sentences. 惟 means joy, 恍 means ecstasy, and 惚 means ecstasy, so altogether, 惟恍惟惚 means ecstasy.

大道廢, 有仁義。
智慧出, 有大偽。
(Chapter 18)

What Laozi would mean is as follows.

The great Tao, universal sexuality, brings the world of inexhaustible supreme bliss and harmony with the essential source. How is it possible for people to be in harmony with each other without this as a base? I cannot help but say that people are just stupid—those who try to harmonize their relationships with only the tip of the head while the essential source remains lost. All of the falseness of human beings comes from the wisdom which has lost this essential source.

Mr. M explained how he reached this great Tao:

"People in civilized societies call a certain feeling a feeling of oneness with all things; however, it is not, in fact, a 'feeling.' When the Tao (sexual relationship) with all things begins, exchange among all things happens. This exchanging condition is followed by the feeling of supreme bliss which is unable to be verbalized. Therefore, this feeling of supreme bliss is not a conceptual 'feeling.' It is a flow of energy, and a transformation of both sides which happens at the same time by co-moving. The condition of recognition of this co-moving is this feeling of supreme bliss. The genuine harmony is created only by the co-moving which has sprung like this from the essential resource."

"The great Tao (大道)" which Laozi taught is not a vague and abstract opinion like "the essential way of human beings." He directly taught the genuine and essential resource.

All things in nature are always led by this great Tao. Therefore, they maintain complete harmony.

Mr. M also recited the words of Laozi to me as follows.

"Do you understand
why flowers in a field are so beautiful?
It is because they talk with the wind,
they talk with the other flowers,
and they are in mutual sympathy with all things.
Then they are filled with supreme bliss.
Do you understand
why children are filled with joy, so innocently?
It is because
they don't have any plans as adults do,
but they are flexible and adaptable
as all things in nature are.
Listen to me well.
Delight is flowing.
Brightness is mutual sympathy.
They are the deepest excitement.
All things are flowing
and in mutual sympathy with each other.
Therefore, all are filled with joy."

"載營魄抱一。能無離乎。
專氣致柔。能嬰兒乎。"
(Chapter 10)

"Look at a woman who reaches ecstasy.
She is filled with the supreme bliss throughout her body,
She is in a void,
and wrapped with the feeling of oneness.
She is in a great love.
A great flow in a void happens within her.
This is one sign.
When you genuinely reach the Tao,
this condition becomes normal."

44

"天門開闔。能爲雌乎。
明白四達。能無知乎。"
(Chapter 10)

He spoke further.

"Civilized people think that sexuality is one part of the human being. This is a big mistake. Sexuality is not one part of the human being. Rather the human being is one part of sexuality.
Civilized people think that sexuality is one part of life's activities. However, sexuality is not one part of life's activities.
Life's activities are only one part of sexuality. Sexuality is not originated from life. It exists before life.
When you observe sexuality, you will know human beings, because the essence of human beings is sexuality.
When you master sexuality, you will understand the universe, because the essence of the universe is sexuality."

His words were like poems.

When you enter forests, the invisible Tao takes place of its own accord between the trees in the forests and yourselves. This is the intrinsic state of human beings, he says. Human beings were originally able to communicate with all living beings. These figures of human beings were sublime existences that will again be actualized only when we return to the original sexual dimension. Even if we insist there is peace, as long as we are apart from such dimensions, it is impossible to achieve, he said.

We put too much on verbalizing words, so we might have forgotten the communication that all these things have. I thought that it might be the result of modern human beings being out of harmony with nature.

Chapter 6

The sexual universe

—The supreme bliss of sexual relations is a pseudo-experience in which the nature of universal source is expressed in lives.

The supreme bliss of the sexual relations brings humans into the genuine psychic universe. It lights up in the subconsciousness of people who have gone astray, and makes them think that human beings must be able to live with a happier feeling. It is a guide to the invisible sub-conscious world... That is the book of "Laozi."

I was taken to the small temple by Mr. M almost every day, and continued learning the esoteric rituals of Laozi little by little.

As I mentioned before, the "Tao" of Laozi is the secret word which means sexuality.

However, this is not the only key word coded in *the book of "Laozi."*

There is another secret word coded as a fellow of "the Tao 道."

That is "the Te 德[7]."

"The Tao 道" means "sexuality," and also means "male genital organs." Comparable to this, the coded word as Shakuji is "Te 德," which means "female genital organs."

Then, what is the original character of this?

---

[7] Common meanings of the "Te" are virtue, moral, excellence, merit, and so on.

Mr. M wrote the character with the brush and showed it to me.
The character was "寶" pronounced "Te."

The meaning of this character was "a round hole." It was a secret
word at that time, meaning the female genital organs, Mr. M said.

This word is used, for example, as follows.

孔德之容, 惟道是從。
道之爲物, 惟恍惟惚。
惚兮恍兮, 其中有象。
恍兮惚兮, 其中有物。
窈兮冥兮, 其中有精。
(Chapter 21)

The formal meaning is as follows.

Figures (容) of people (德) of the great (孔) Tao (道)
the truth (道) of origin.
The Tao creates a clear world
from the vague and faint (惟恍惟惚) dimension.
In the very great depth (窈兮冥兮)
mysterious activities (精) take place.

However, if I translate the secret meaning directly, it is as follows.

The vessel of the hole (孔) of the female genital organ (德)
follows the pokes of the male genital organ (道).
When the male genital organ pokes,
the female genital organ falls into ecstasy
and leaves all things to take their own course.
When the male genital organ emits sperm (精),
the female genital organ just accepts them in ecstasy.
In the very ecstasy,
sperm is emitted
into the deep and mysterious hole (窈兮冥兮).

From there he tries to catch a glimpse of the most sacred dimension in the universe.

These are the next phrases:

其精甚眞, 其中有信。
自古及今, 其名不去, 以閱衆甫。
吾何以知衆甫之状哉。以此。

I see the highest truth
in the depth of this sexual phenomenon,
which is undeniably creative.
The essence of immutable heaven is there.
The essence is beyond time,
and it is also the power to rule over all things.
The reason
why I understand all the rules
is that I observe all things
in the depth of this sexual activity.

The book of "Laozi" reveals a combination of the formal meanings with the secret meanings. This is not accidental.

If I freely translate the genuine meaning of Laozi from both of them, it is as follows.

A man of real virtue is a man who surrenders himself
to the teaching of the Tao.
He becomes like a woman
who surrenders herself to her man.
As the woman is implanted with sperm
in a pleasant feeling of ecstasy,
a person in the supreme bliss
is shaken by the essential wisdom (精) in the universe
and trembles with its pleasure.
As a small spermatozoon builds a human body without mistake,

> the invisible wisdom (精)
> leads all things as they should be.
> This wisdom (精) is the very eternal and unchangeable essence,
> which is beyond all other phenomena.
> The reason why I understand all the rules
> is due to this holy spirit (精),
> which is beyond sexual energy (精).[8]

According to Mr. M, all animals and plants in nature establish their essence in ecstasy. Therefore, we human beings also have to set our goals in this "ecstasy," he says. I was shocked by this point of view, which was completely different from my own view of life up to this time.

He said:

> "Do you see that the beautiful flowers in their full bloom secrete honey, enjoying their feelings of ecstasy when they do it?
> The butterflies come to them, also pulled by ecstasy. Or rather, they achieve such activities exactly because they can be in ecstasy. It is similar to the ecstasy in which a woman obtains continuous joy in her whole body, and also similar to the children's hearts which are free when born. Only in the hearts of ecstasy like this, are people full of new vigor, creative energy, and infinitive love."

By the way, if forced to listen to the secret meanings of *the book of "Laozi,"* eminent people might say,

> "Can the word 'Tao,' which should preach the way of human beings, mean sex, of all things?
> Besides, is ecstasy the essence of human beings?
> What an immoral thinker!"

---

[8] The letter 精 has various meanings as Chinese letters have in general, for example, spirit, wisdom, energy, vigor, and sperm.

People at the time of Laozi would also have considered these thoughts to be immoral if the genuine intention of Laozi had been openly expressed.

However, according to the teachings of Laozi, what they value the most, namely "Tao Te 道德" itself, means the coniunctio between the male genital organ (Tao 道) and the female one (Te 德)!

This coded expression is a skillful irony.

Laozi wanted to say as follows behind this expression.

"The Tao Te (道德[9]) that you insist is superficial, as if it were blown by the wind.
Human beings must live in a way more rooted to the earth."

He may be murmuring.

"Do you know the most stable foundation rooted to the earth for human beings?
That is what you dare not to see.
It is what you are afraid to talk about the most.
All things begin from there, however,
why do you try to protect your eyes from it?
The truth which harmonizes all things lies
behind the very thing that you are afraid of.
True life cannot be fulfilled without knowing it.
All truth of the way of human life is within this."

The present world is jammed with people who search for success in life, status and power. It might be like a traffic jam in an urban city. Some might happen to meet accidents and other might be able to proceed further than the others. However, they commonly live in an irritable world psychically, which is the farthest thing from "ecstasy." And, because of their hearts, they hurt both themselves and others.

---

[9] A common meaning of the "Tao Te" as a two-character compound is morality.

This is the figure of people, which has not been changed from the time of Laozi. The representative word to show the best condition of human beings are "the Tao Te 道德," "the virtuous character 德性," "the Te (virtue)德" and "the Tao 道," all of which were used willingly by people who aimed at acquiring power.

The book of "Laozi" is also called *the Tao Te Ching of "Laozi"* (老子道德經).

This is because two words "the Tao 道" and "the Te 德" are mentioned quite a lot in *the book of "Laozi"* and we can even say that *the book of "Laozi"* is a book about "the Tao 道" and "the Te 德." Besides, *the book of "Laozi"* consists of two parts, and sometimes the first part is called "the Tao Ching[10] (a sutra of the Tao) 道經" and the second part "the Te Ching (a sutra of the virtue) 德經," because the first one begins with "the Tao 道" and the second one does with "the Te 德." Altogether it is called "the Tao Te Ching (a sutra of the morality) 道德經."

Laozi concealed his calculatedly skilled code to describe the sexual relationship with the words "the Tao Te (morality) 道德" which people so valued. The name of the book *The Tao Te Ching of "Laozi"* (老子道德經) means in fact "Laozi's sutras on the sexual relationship." What a sense of humor he had!

People in authority try to create harmony among people through superficial and artistic behavior. This was based on the morality symbolized in "Tao Te (道德)." It also maintained the power of people in authority in China at that time. Confucian ideas were spread throughout the world. Laozi actually made cynical remarks about the words which authoritative people liked, while using his excellent code!

First of all, we should have noticed that it was strange for Laozi to use this word so often since it must have been a word he didn't like, Mr. M said.

He dared to choose this word to teach the truth.

---

[10] A common meaning of the "Ching" is a sutra. So, the meaning of "the Tao Ching" is a sutra of the Tao.

On one hand, "the Tao 道" is the cord of the sexual relationship and the male genital organ, on the other hand, "the Te 德" is the code of the female genital organ. Understanding these two is the only way to dispel doubts about what Laozi wanted to teach behind *the book of "Laozi,"* which is very ambiguous.

"The Te 德" means "the essence of a man who masters "the Tao 道" in general, as the words "a priest of great virtue (高徳の僧)[11]" shows. However, Laozi concealed the excellent secret teachings of sexuality in code behind this word.

The meaning of "the Te 德" that he wanted to express in code is "a female genital organ which accepts a male genital organ."

Normal people would not be able to connect "a man who masters the Tao 道" with "a female genital organ which accepts a male genital organ" at all.

However, both can be connected as one in his mind. This is because the Tao 道 for Laozi means oneness with the universe, and the sexual relationship, by which a person becomes one with the other sex temporarily, is filled with symbolism which brings about a pseudo-body-feeling of oneness with the universe.

Laozi understood intuitively that the words suggest various truths at the same time.

The female genital organ itself does not conceive a life on its own. It takes the male genital organ to make it conceive.

He knew intuitively that this principle is a model of the principle of humanity and earth. The universe is a systematic substance. It has an extraordinarily finely tuned order. Compared to it, the brain of a human being is so poor that it cannot create even a vestige of life. All things in the universe faithfully follow this extraordinary wisdom, and complete perfect harmony by themselves. Laozi saw a symbol of this infinite wisdom within the movement of the male genital organ (spermatozoa). Within the female genital organ, met by the male genital organ, the universe surrenders all to extraordinary wisdom.

---

[11] 高 means "great", の means "of", and 僧 means "priest."

This is a fundamental principle of the universe, and Laozi knew it intuitively.

"A man who masters the Tao 道" means, according to him, a man who accepts not his own small will, but the infinite wisdom as it is, as the universe does.

Sexuality is the other self of the wisdom of the universe itself. Therefore, all things are born from the ultimate sexuality. Each cell, each molecule, and each atom are born of sexuality, Laozi would say.

Electrons go around an atomic nucleus, and atoms meet each other. They are a kind of love and sexual relationship. The atoms are not only moving, but also enjoying their movement. They are doing it for the pleasure. Behind such minute movements as pleasure, the great Tao (大道) is concealed. It surpasses all of them, supervises them, and it is an activity which is invisible. It is the only infinite wisdom, and the eternal Tao (常道).

Laozi expressed this movement of the universe splendidly with the single character "the Te 德."

Mr. M said, "The essence of wisdom is ecstasy." He means that we should entrust ourselves with this wisdom of the universe as the female genital organs do.

Laozi also often used the word "玄德."

"玄" means "profound."

By this word "玄德," namely, "the profound female genital organs," he shows the existence which is shaken by the wisdom of the profound universe, and indicates that people can reach for the greatest pleasure only through it.

天門開闔, 能爲雌乎。
明白四達, 能無知乎。
生之畜之, 生而不有。
爲而不恃, 長而不宰。
是謂玄德。
(Chapter 10)

Look at a woman who reaches ecstasy,
with her genital organ opening and closing.
Her whole body is filled with the supreme bliss
and she becomes one with the world in every direction,
and feels and masters all things,
however, she is an existence of being free from anything.
A life is born in such a condition.
She, who is unified with heaven and earth,
brings up her child warmly,
but does not possess it.
Whatever she does well,
she doesn't boast of it,
nor is she proud that she is loved.
The very figure of such a woman is the mystic woman,
namely, "the profound female 玄德."

He says that an individual who is shaken by the wisdom of the universe doesn't seek to fulfill his own interests as the men of power do, because he is filled with the supreme bliss, the same as a woman in ecstasy.

It is not only this character "the Te 德" that Laozi uses as a code of the female genital organ.

When he says "門 (gate)," this is also a code word for the same thing.

When he uses the character "門 (gate)," he intends to show an entrance to the great Tao at the same time.

He also uses the character "谷 (valley)" as a code of the female genital organ.

When he uses the letter "谷 (valley)," his concurrent intention is to show the creativity that is born from the great receptivity of a valley receiving the downward flow of water. This is because, like the female genital organ which accepts the Tao 道, that is, the male genital organ, all of creation has boundless receptivity of the Tao, and the true creation is born from this receptivity.

Laozi pays attention to the female genital organ and has a belief in the femininity behind it. And by using it as a medium, he tries to talk about the meaning of the principle of motherhood, which has been lost in the society of manhood.

He says,

谷神不死，
是謂玄牝[12]。
玄牝之門，
是謂天地根。
綿綿若存，
用之不勤。
(Chapter 6)

It is said that the God that dwells in a great 'valley' has an eternal life.
This is called "the 玄牝" (profound female),
namely, a mystic woman.
The gate of the mystic woman
is the very fundamental activity of heaven and earth.
It bears all things for ever.
However many you use, they will never be used up.

知其雄，
守其雌，
爲天下谷。
爲天下谷，
常德[13]不離，
復歸嬰兒。
(Chapter 28)

---

[12] 玄＝profound, 牝＝雌＝female
[13] 常德 is an antithesis of the eternal Tao 常道. The world of eternal supreme bliss.

You should first know what sort of thing
masculinity (the male principle) is.
When you truly understand it,
you will see how close to heaven
femininity (the female principle) is.
When you become the embodiment of femininity,
everybody is attracted
and all things flow into you
as water flows into a valley.
Then you become one
with the rhythm of all things in nature,
in the supreme bliss like a small child.
This is called the universal "Te (德)."

Laozi was a believer in femininity. However, he didn't mean that
women were good and men were not. He talked intelligibly about the
Yin-Yang principle of heaven and earth by replacing it with the world
of human beings. He tried to make us notice that people living in
a society with a one-sided orientation towards masculinity were in
opposition to the principles of nature.

All things occur in the reciprocal actions of Yin and Yang, Laozi
said.

道生一，
一生二，
二生三，
三生萬物。
萬物負陰而抱陽。
(Chapter 42)

The Tao produced one,
the one developed into two, Yin and Yang,
and the Yin and the Yang had intercourse
to produce all things.

Therefore, all things have their Yin outside,
and embrace the Yang inside.

The Yin-Yang theory of Laozi, which Dr. Hideki Yukawa, who won the Nobel prize for physics, also used as a foundation for his own ideas, doubtlessly describes something just like an atomic structure. However, this truth also shows the phenomenon of mixing male and female, which relates to Laozi's ideas, and symbolizes the universal rule of all things, as he himself wrote in Chapter 21.

反者道之動,
弱者道之用。
天下萬物生於有,
有生於無。
(Chapter 40)

All things are created
by a reciprocal action of its opposite,
such as an active activity (Yang)
like a male genital organ
bent backwards strongly, on the one hand,
and a passive activity (Yin),
like a female genital organ
accepting it softly, on the other hand.

Not limited to human beings and life,
all things in this world are produced
by reciprocal actions (an object's activity to produce another object) like this.

And the essence,
which produces such reciprocal action,
is the very great Tao,
which surpasses relativity.

According to Laozi, this reciprocal action of Yin and Yang is the result of ecstasy on a universal scale.

Therefore, we human beings are also held by the actions of Yin and Yang, namely, male and female.

Every human wishes to be in sympathy with his or her beloved. "How happy I would be, if I could do so..." People keep looking for such a relationship no matter how difficult it is to find. From where does this impulse come? People seek love not only from a beloved. Why do people keep seeking love?

What, indeed, are we looking for?

Laozi stared at the object we seek most strongly, but which we cannot understand because it is so deep and huge. He tried to make us focus on the psychic universe that is too huge to grasp, by using the most appropriate lens, namely, sexuality.

Many people talk about "love." Everyone from intellectuals to saints often talk about "love." However, I feel we have not been able to make its essence clear, even though we talk about it often.

Besides, even today, it is not proper to discuss sexuality in public. However, Laozi clearly indicated the essence of the universe by referring to love using the lens of "sexuality."

Ultimate love, which everybody seeks, is the great Tao; that is, it is a sphere that is influenced by a wave of the supreme bliss where all things are created. People continue to look for it without knowing its true character. Once a saint said that "God is love." This may be what everybody is searching for unconsciously. This supreme bliss is usually impossible to realize unless the consciousness matches its sphere. However, the sexual experience of human beings gives us supreme bliss for a little while. Laozi named it "the Tao 道," the guide to the world for which human beings should aim. The guide was given to humanity long before Laozi wrote it down. He was the one who realized it first. Sexual ecstasy is supreme bliss that everybody experiences. It is the only common language of supreme bliss for all humanity.

Laozi realized that sexual ecstasy was a pseudo-experience in which the pulsating motion of the universe itself is expressed, and it is a moment in which human beings temporarily act out the activity of the universe itself.

Sexual ecstasy, however, is over in a moment. Compared to this, the feeling of oneness with all things, the original activity of the universe itself, is a never-ending feeling of supreme bliss. It is the ecstasy of all existence, which is beyond the partial ecstasy felt in the sexual organs, and in which all of cells of the body shiver with joy.

Laozi knew the world of unchangeable supreme bliss.

He was probably the first man in the history of humanity, who dared to say that the world of unchangeable supreme bliss has some aspects in common with the sexual experience.

He sealed it with a wonderful code, and succeeded in hiding it from the people in authority.

No matter which part you read, you will find no expressions of sexuality in *the book of "Laozi."* Yet, it describes the truth of sexuality in a two-fold structure behind the text.

The supreme bliss of sexual relations brings humans into the genuine psychic universe. It lights up in the sub-consciousness of people who have gone astray, and makes them think that human beings must be able to live with a happier feeling. It is a guide to the invisible sub-conscious world. The book that is written with this excellent description, which combines the two sides of Yin and Yang, namely sexuality and the true way of life, and the book in which the way of expression itself is taken wonderfully into account to show how humanity should live on earth, is *the book of "Laozi."*

Chapter 7

Sexuality and human society

—The moment when sexuality is diverted from the essence of the universe and transforms into desire.

"Do you know why Laozi sets his sights on sexuality so much?
It is because without sexuality, there are neither human transformations nor social.
Sexuality is not only the essence of humans, but also the essence of society, and of the universe."

The more time passes, the more something in me is washed out, I feel. That something might be like stains accumulated unnoticed by the wind of modern society.

It seemed that Mr. M had a great deal of knowledge about civilized society.

He said,

"I have experienced modern civilized society only for a short period. I know that it has unhappiness which we don't have in our village. And I understand where it comes from.
Sexuality is not only the origin of life, but also the pulsating motion of the universe itself. When it acts with this motion, sexuality is no longer merely a desire. Only by being diverted from the rhythm of the universe, does it turn into desire.

That which draws sexuality apart from the pulsating motion of the universe is society going against the rhythm of nature. The sexual expression and sexual desires of modern people are directly connected to inharmonious social functions. A concept forms a social function, and the social function forms a concept among people. The concept and sexuality are as connected as are two sides of a car's wheel. The sexual subconscious alone forms a whole concept of a person. In turn, a concept decides the way of sexuality. In this way, a social system and sexuality are like two sides of a wheel. A change on one side necessarily causes a transformation of the other."

He said further.

"In an era when feudal society broke down and people tried to make a new society, there was a change in the concept of sexuality and its customs. This happened before functional changes in society. First of all, feudal sexuality began to collapse. Then advanced people began to seek a new form of intimate relationship between males and females. It was the first step in making overall changes. Society then changed rapidly, and people became dissatisfied with the system of feudal society itself. The concept changed, and the function reached actual transformation.

Do you know why Laozi sets his sights on sexuality so much? It is because without sexuality, there are neither human transformations nor social.

Sexuality is not only the essence of humans, but also the essence of society, and of the universe."

It is written in the sacred book of Judaism, *the Talmud,*[14] "All things about a person are understood by the way of sexual activities of the

---

[14] Talmud (meaning of "research") is another law of Moses. According to the Jewish tradition,

person." I could not have imagined why such a thing was written in a book of religious teachings. However, as I came in contact with Mr. M, I began to understand the deep meanings of such words.

If I restate it in the way of Mr. M, we can say the following:

"All things about a society can be understood by the sexual activities of the people in the society."

The more I knew about Mr. M, the more mysterious he seemed.

I wanted to know more fundamentally about human beings, but this was not the sort of thing taught at school. I had studied philosophy, religion, and psychology to understand, but I was not satisfied with Japanese experts and books in these spheres, and something continued to smolder within me. The very something that I wanted to know, he had in himself, this I began to feel.

Well, one day, Mr. M finally told me about a secret of his village.

"There is a legend of Laozi passed down in my family."

It was an unexpected story.

The story went back thousands of years. The head of a village in the south part of China became acquainted with a minority ethnic group, and married a daughter of the leader of the group. Then a boy was born, and was later named Laozi. He was brought up influenced by both the Chinese culture, which was civilized on a large scale at that time, and the culture of the smaller ethnic group.

As he grew up in this environment, he began to feel at home in the culture of the minority group. He lived in Luoyang in the center of China, and at that time, learned about the unpleasant aspects of

---

God gave Moses the written law (the written Torah) and also the oral law (the oral Torah). This oral law is Talmud. Many of the major modern Judaism denominations recognize it as the Scripture, and the faith and life of Jews are based on it. It is believed to have reaches its current form in the 6th century.

Chinese society; he became more certain of the cultural value of the ethnic group in which he was raised.

He was a born thinker, respected while he lived with his mother's people, eventually becoming the oldest of them. For the sake of his progeny, and to protect the ancient culture, he wrote the truth in a book that was passed down. It became the model for *the book of "Laozi"* of today.

By the way, the province Unnan is a region where many ethnic groups continue to live. In the old days, they probably had most of the world to themselves.

I can understand that *the book of "Laozi"* looks like a cultural model of the minority group. Probably Laozi hoped to bring the culture back to life as a home for all humanity, not just his own descendants.

It was said that Laozi was asked by some thoughtful people in Chinese society to give lectures, and sometimes did so. Laozi must have cut a brilliant figure in China.

Mr. M said that *the book of "Laozi,"* which was well known in the present world, contained many verses added later by Taoist scholars among the Han Chinese, who didn't understand the genuine intention of Laozi well enough. Thus, the style was different from that of the original book of "Laozi." *The book of "Laozi"* which was passed down in the village of Mr. M was only one-third the length of that of known today. It must be the original one.

Twenty years after this experience, I visited the village of the Long-Neck people in Thailand.

Long-Neck people live in an area not far[15] from the border of the province Yunnan where Laozi's village was. The two villages had a lot in common, and there were many beautiful women in the tribe as well.

However, what astonished me in the quiet village in the deep jungle was that there was a "school" that was only a small hut. Thai

---

[15] In a Japanese version, it is described as closer than the distance between Tokyo and Nagoya, ca. 370 km.

language was taught at this school that the Thai government built, and children of the Long-Neck people began to gradually speak Thai, until they were in danger of losing their original language. This is just one of the phenomena that has happened in the world. Some civilized people try to discover the value of a culture native to the land, but they end up destroying it completely. Wherever culture meets government, the government always wins, and the natives are assimilated into the country. However, the reverse condition happened in this village.

According to Mr. M, people in the mountain village where my friend brought me before were offspring of the Chinese (the Han race) who were strongly attracted to Laozi a long time ago. It is said that they moved into the deep mountains to escape civilization and follow Laozi. It was a miraculous social phenomenon.

The religion, which was based on the idea of Laozi among the Han race, was called Taoism. However, the Taoism of the Han race, in general, was the people's original beliefs, and to which beliefs (after Laozi) were added. On the other hand, I was taught that the mountain village was the only place where people genuinely protected Laozi's way of thinking.

Laozi's way of thinking was very close to the people of anti-government circles. At that time in China, civilization advanced and national power was strong. The state did its best to use the people as its source of economy and as its fighting power. Human relationships of ancient times were lost and culture disappeared. What were left were human beings controlled by the national government. Laozi, who saw through the situation, allowed his followers to live near his village.

The figure of Mr. M, who went back and forth from the mountain village to this village, and was attached to the villagers in both, was a recreation of the figure of Laozi.

Chapter 8

The sexual dimension that decides all courses

—Divinity or desire? Which is the way to reach "the dimension of eternal happiness"?

> ". . . *sexuality was originally far from indecent, it was just the opposite. . .*
> *There is an energy which lets human beings attain all things they need.*
> *There is an ultimate universe which goes beyond the frame of humanity, and goes farther beyond the limitations of life."*

The more contact I had with Mr. M, the more I felt myself come closer to my true self. The closer I came to my true self, the more I felt I understood the genuine intentions of *the book of "Laozi."* Furthermore, the more I understood *the book of "Laozi,"* the more I realized how ideal this village was.

There was one question I had had since I came to this village, but I have not mentioned it yet. There was a custom of what civilized people would regard as a religious belief in genital organs.

In this village, the entrance of a house was regarded as a female organ. A wood shaped like the female genital organ is put at the entrance of some houses, and villagers greet the symbol every morning and evening with the same movements (prayer) as they do to the spirits of flowers. In addition, a figure shaped like a male genital organ is placed at the center of every house as a symbol of the spirits. (A fireplace acts as a substitute for it in some houses.)

If our houses had such symbols, we would consider them indecent, and look away from them as if they were something shameful. However, the villagers put such sexual symbols not only in public spaces, but also in their most sacred places. It would be a proof that they did not have the slightest feeling that sexuality was indecent. They accepted sexuality and recognized it in a way that is completely different from the way we do.

Mr. M once told me as follows.

"It is no wonder that every child considers his mother and father, who protect him, as gods.

A child does not feel that his mother is 'like' a god, but believes she actually is one. When the child is directing his attention to his mother, he intuitively knows that motherhood itself is as a part of the universe.

Motherhood in this universe functions in a much larger and profound sphere than you feel. It is limitless. You are guided by motherhood and fatherhood to the degree to which your soul is guided by them. As the child resembles its father and mother, an image of recognition of its own sacredness itself becomes a vessel to cultivate the person. That is the reason why we always hang the symbols of the male genital organ as well as the female genital organ within our sight. In the depth of them we see a much huger world than you can recognize. It is called God.

The essence of motherhood and fatherhood is the eternal Tao 常道. The importance of it is that such permanent sacredness dwells within you, too. Sacred motherhood and sacred fatherhood are transcendent. In fact, your existence itself is sacred. Then, when you are, and meet another similar existence, it is a true encounter of male and female, just as the universe intends. Never forget this."

Through such experiences I began to notice that this was the village where the ideals of Laozi were realized as they were meant to be. I felt that the world he expressed in his code was actualized in the village. However, at the next moment, I suddenly remembered one thing.

To my surprise, the village was very similar to types of villages that existed in Japan until the Meiji Era.[16]

They regarded some objects shaped like the genital organs as symbols of God, and the objects were worshipped by every family in various places. For example, the Kofu region[17] is famous for genital worship. It was the very origin of belief before the Jyomon era,[18] a time that preceded Buddhist temples and Shinto shrines.

However, these beliefs were regarded as heathen customs, so they were forbidden by the Meiji government, the first Western style government in Japan. The precious inheritance that most likely had lasted for several thousand or even several tens of thousands of years was cut off at that moment, and seemed destined to disappear completely. I knew such cultures were remnants from ancient times in Japan. However, I am ashamed to say that I just thought of them as primitive superstitions. After I came to this village and touched its living culture, I was overwhelmed by the depth of its insight. I was ashamed of my prejudices. At the same time, I was rather surprised by the depth of my culture, and understood that Japanese culture should be maintained. Back in Japan, I searched for the precious inheritance of which so little is left, and got a chance to take photos that I would like you to see.[19] They show how sincerely ancient Japanese people connected with sexuality. I would like the readers to accept the following facts deeply. These people on the Japanese archipelago who believed in God with all their hearts lost their beliefs to the Meiji government.

When I came to this village, Mr. M asked me once as follows.

---

[16] Meiji Era: 1868-1912
[17] Kofu region: the mountainous district in central Japan
[18] Jyomon Era: ca. 30 B.C.–10 B.C.
[19] Photos are offered by private collection of Amano family. See page 129.

"There is a standard with which we can judge whether a society is able to accept the essential happiness of human beings. What do you think it is?"

I was perplexed as to the answer. He continued,

"It is whether society accepts sexuality, or fights against it.
You in the civilized society think that sexuality is indecent. You avoid talking about it in public as much as possible. Once you mention it, your dignity is doubted. This is how you think of sexuality. You regard it as an object of suppression, and believe that sexual desires are troublesome. You think that suppressing sexual desires and not talking about them is kindness.
You have forgotten that sexuality is originally not indecent, but rather the opposite. However, what made it indecent was a ruler who appeared in your society; it was that power, and also a concept of good and evil made by such authorities. If you open your eyes and see things as they are, you find everything you need in sexuality. Sexuality is natural because it is the source of life and the center of the abundance of nature. There is an energy which lets human beings reach for what we need. There is an ultimate universe which goes beyond the framework of humanity and beyond the limitations of life. Human beings can reach for eternal happiness only through genuine sexuality."

"Sexuality" harmonizes with nature, and has the power to decide whether all people in society can enjoy essential happiness. It might have been a clear strategy by the Meiji government to thoroughly suppress beliefs in sexuality and completely destroy it.

Why does modern society dare not to accept sexuality?

Sexuality has a great commercial function in society. The majority of magazines lined up in book shops trigger consciousness of sexual matters, directly or indirectly. Even beauty and fashion are connected to sexual consciousness. The more distorted and suppressed the consciousness of sexual matters, the greater its attraction.

In a society open to sexuality, people do not seek it immoderately. In such a case, commerce would become stagnant. Statistics show that a single man, who earns more than the average income, consumes more than half of his disposable income on sex or things related to sex. Female wishes for love and beauty, when considered aspects of sexuality, are even greater than sexual needs of men.

The rulers in both commercial and authoritarian societies in any era tend to attach weight to suppressing sexuality. "You should paint only this part of the genitals of this nude, then you can sell it..." Why don't they forbid all nudes? Why don't they accept all of them? Why do they despise the most sublime part of living creatures? Why is it a sin to be as we were born?

The result of all this is an increase in sexual desires. Freud, said that sexual desires existed at the bottom of human impulse. This has one aspect of truth. Laozi also indicates indirectly that all desires of human beings are connected to the repressed consciousness of sexual matters at the bottom of human psyche.

People who are swelled with desire pursue money, many other items of value, and happiness. They cannot see the fortune given by God as it is, and they keep seeking for money and other valuables as distorted substitutes for what they desire. The very activity activates the economy. Desires move people and the society. They become the very center of principles. As the formative principle of feudal society was within humanity and justice, the formative principle of modern society is part of the concept of desire. This concept undermines the natural world as it seeks for wealth and power, and then results in people fighting each other. Desires are never satisfied by being pursued, and they know no limitations. Eventually, distortions bear even worse distortions. That is the tragedy of modern society.

Compared to people in this village who extract divinity from humans by focusing on sexuality, our society only increases desire by stimulating consciousness of sexual matters. There is a complete contrast based on whether we aim at desires, or at lofty-mindedness. The essence of the concept is the same, and sexuality is its border.

No one was ashamed of nudity in this village. Children are brought up seeing adults who hold sexuality sacred from their childhood. In my first days there, I happened to meet some women who were bathing in a river. All of them were naked, and I didn't know what to do. I was rather surprised to discover that they were not at all alarmed, and behaved just as usual. Males and females often bathed in a river together. When it was hot, sometimes they spent the day without clothes. Moreover, they had no notion of sexual intercourse being embarrassing. Though I have read that the natives in India have sexual intercourse even in the presence of others, I, of course, had never seen such a thing myself. In the village I saw it several times, and I was amazed to find behavior so completely different from sexual relationships of we civilized people. I will discuss this later in detail. I was convinced by all of this that the villagers had a sexual concept which was completely different from ours, ejaculation for ejaculation's sake, and it came from their reverent attitude toward sexuality.

Children in this village were brought up seeing such scenes as a matter of course.

At first, I too thought that being brought up seeing adults who regard genital organs or sexuality itself as objects of reverence was the most natural and ideal sex education.

However, the more I understood, the more I realized my ideas were inappropriate. To consider their sexual practices as a form of sex education was a conceited way of forcing the values of civilization on the villagers. That is because the concept of teaching something puts more emphasis on the teacher than the subject itself—and that is wrong. There was no room at all for the impudent concept of "teaching" in their hearts. They didn't think of themselves as models. They merely worshipped their deities. The very genuinely modest attitudes toward sexuality are what elevate the children, who are extremely free—beyond the Japanese imagination—and they are as tender as the deities. Their figures showed me what a sick country

Japan is, where even abnormal and queer incidents caused by children or youth are a daily occurrence.

My ideas toward sexuality changed gradually. It was no wonder females were objects of sexual desire in Japan. However, such thoughts disappeared from me unnoticed as I adapted to the society in the village. Female figures with long hair bathing in a river melt into the scenery of great nature; it is so beautiful. I was fascinated by them, and noticed myself staring at them with a different sensitivity from that which I had in Japan.

Chapter 9

Sexual energy and sacred sex

—Greatness of hidden power within our bodies.

...He called this central axis of the human body "the trunk of Tao." It is inside humans as well as all other forms of life, and it can be called the sexual center. . . . The amount of spiritual energy flowing in the sexual center is in proportion to the radiance of the aura from a human body, and it gives off a silent message, he says.

After I came to this village, taking a walk in nature became one of my pleasures.

There was a forest of excellent bamboo about one kilometer from the village. Countless stalks of bamboo rising towards heaven spread over an area of two kilometers, as if protecting the mountains.

Nature that reminds me of southern countries is nice. However, this bamboo forest filled with oriental mystery was much more attractive to me.

Partway down a small hill, I found an open space around 20 meters in diameter in this bamboo field. It was cool there surrounded by the bamboo and made me feel as easy as if I were in a house made by nature. It became my favorite place to go.

When I was walking on a narrow path to go to this "house in the bamboo forest," I sensed a sign of something very special. While I lived in this village, I became sensitive to signs, and I sensed a certain sign as I came close to the house at that time, too.

When I came to the "house in the bamboo forest," I sensed that a person was there. It was a man who looked to be in his late twenties. He was almost complete naked and stood still with one hand raised, his other arm stretching toward the back, twisting his body in a spiral, and looking backwards. I felt that there was a flow of strong energy within the twisted and stretched-back muscle. The space surrounded by this bamboo forest felt completely differently from usual.

What on earth was it?

I was filled with an impulse to know the meaning of his activity. I had met him once in the village. He was only a villager who lived a normal life. Here, in this mysterious place, however, he seemed to be a human who transcended humanity.

Aside from communication with the spirits I mentioned before, the villagers did something like gymnastics or prayers such as I had never seen in Japan. I cannot find any other words to express their activities. However, it was not the sort of gymnastics we might imagine. For example, the villagers raised their hands upwards, and stood still for several minutes in this posture, with the palm of their hands facing toward the heavens. When the sun rose in the morning, I often saw villagers meditating. My first impression was that the prayer-like activity was in a completely different dimension from ours.

Later I was taught by the villagers that this was called "Yahma."

I was also taught by Mr. M that the practice had continued since time immemorial.

Many movements were silent and still, however, there was a sharp movement in which, from the posture of bending forward languidly, they stretched out one of their hands towards heaven, while breathing with a "whoosh." According to Mr. M, "Yahma" essentially means behaviors that receive humans as spirits.

According to his explanation, our incarnations as spirits mean sexual energy. The reason why women in this village who do this

Yahma are so attractive in everyday life would be that sexual energy enhances their sexual attraction, and it lasts throughout their lives.

We civilized people tend to look down on original cultures as underdeveloped. However, every time I meet such unknown cultures, I feel that this notion is nothing but arrogant prejudice. This meeting with Yahma was typical of such an experience.

Mr. M said that ancestors in this village might have a connection to the original culture of India. If I reflect on it, Yahma looks similar to yoga. I learned later that yoga was not developed by the existing Indian Aryans, but originally performed by the Dravidian, namely, the people who first inhabited India. The Aryans excel in thinking logically, so they systematized it within their own culture later. The Dravidians were divided into several hundred tribes. They might have kept such a physical culture in each small tribe. They originated from the Sumer culture, regarded as the first civilization of human beings. They built the Indus civilization, and after it disappeared, their offspring moved to the East, Mr. M told me. Yahma may be very close to yoga before it was influenced by the Aryans, and its origin might go back to the Sumer people.

(I also found later that a physical culture similar to it was known among the original inhabitants of the vast area from western to eastern Asia, though it was not systematized as much as yoga. The common point among the many tribes was that their language had the same structure as Japanese language in which a noun is followed by a participle.)

Observing the villagers silently doing Yahma made me feel that human beings are the greatest works of art. This beauty comes from the essential nature that is shown when people are incarnations of spirits.

Throughout the bamboo forest are places suited to doing Yahma. I hear that doing it alone or in a group have different meanings. Doing it alone in nature helps one to receive a spiritual aura.

The figure of the man looked mysterious with the background of the beautiful bamboo forest. It could have a stage for the tale *The*

Moon Princess.[20] The man was still, however, and I felt energy flowing through his body. It seemed as though the energy was a vertical flow down his backbone—in splendid harmony with the bamboo forest.

According to Mr. M, this mutual sympathy between the different sorts of life in nature expands the fundamental sphere of human consciousness. When males and females love each other genuinely, they experience the mutual sympathy of supreme bliss between opposite sexes. Similar mutual sympathy is possible in every form of life. The more heterogeneous the object, the more universal the sphere of supreme bliss becomes and the more essential and deeper its quality, said Mr. M.

We in civilized society try to expedite the progress of physical abilities and mental faculties. Compared to this, I thought that the culture in the village attached importance to progress of fundamental consciousness. It was this lifestyle that gave the people in the village dignity, as well as remarkable beauty and expressiveness.

Several times I saw women doing Yahma naked. It was as if they were in silent, nude ecstasy communicating with plants and bamboos in the forest. As they moved, birds often appeared and began to slowly circle over them. When I was wondering if it was a mere accident, Mr. M taught me that it was a sign of blessing. When sexual energy was activated, and an invisible energetic whirlpool was formed even in the sky, at this sign, the birds followed the energy, he said. It sounded incredible but appeared to be true.

The suppleness of the women's bodies was amazing, and everybody was soft. Children also enjoyed jumping and flipping like acrobats when they got together in this open space. The girls impressed me strongly with their notion that when they stretched a certain part of their bodies, the stretched part became a place where spirits appeared.

They said that the purpose of every style of Yahma is to set a place on the body for the spirits to appear. For example, they moved

---

[20] "*The Moon Princess*" is a Japanese fairy tale. The princess was born out of a bamboo tube in a bamboo forest.

in a way similar to us when they bent forward. But they handled their bodies in ways unrecognizable by us. They did not bend at the joints, but let the energy of spirits in nature appear by stretching the bottoms of their feet and their backs. The spirit they spoke of was natural energy, wisdom, and the invisible work of God.

It is said that the energy flow along the backbone arises in this way, and it extends even outside of the body, just as I felt when I saw the man in the forest. The girls called this invisible flow of aura the "body of spirits."

To them, spirits and sexual energy are almost the same. They don't see sexual energy as something that involves only a certain spot, like the genitals. For them, the whole body is involved in sexuality, and the whole universe is essentially sexual.

According to Mr. M, stretching our body has a far greater sacred meaning than we imagine. Pulling the body only from one side is not enough, the other side of the body must also be pulled. This results in a phenomenon of stretching. When this action of opposites, which can be regarded as Yin and Yang, works in an agreeable way, the spirits begin to work in this material world, he said. Of course, this idea applies to other kinds of Yin and Yang, such as tension and relaxation, and so on. And this is the law that holds true of all things in the whole natural world, he explained.

Another thing in Mr. M's explanation surprised me. It was that, if the spirits dwelled in the stretched part, it meant that wisdom dwelled there too. It would be extremely difficult for modern people to understand this. However, I could not help feeling that it was true, when looking at Mr. M, who gave off an aura of a wise old man. He made me feel that he was very noble as a human being—it was as if all of the cells in his body were made of wisdom. He was completely different from so-called intellectuals in our society. These intellectuals merely cram a lot of knowledge into their heads. Compared to Mr. M, we are poor and unbalanced creatures. He had the figure of one who thought and understood the truth with his whole body. He made me feel the intelligence of a completely different dimension from ours. Deep stillness continuously flowed around him. Silence among people in modern society means decreasing tension between people. In his case, however, it was completely opposite. At the very moment of stillness, it was as if he were speaking volumes. When he was in a deep stillness, some mutual sympathy, something too deep to verbalize, began. I cannot correctly express it. However, I felt as if something like an electric message was sent out in a striking tempo from his body in the stillness.

I was taught by Mr. M that the most important part of the human body was its axis, a point from the crown of the head, and extending directly beneath it. (It seemed to be aligned with the central nerves of the spinal cord.) He called this central axis of the human body "a trunk of Tao." It is inside humans as well as all other forms of life, and it can be called the sexual center. People in the village called this center "La." The brain is at the upper end of this "trunk of Tao," the genital organs are at the lower end of it, and the whole makes up the foundation of a being, he said. The sexual center is also the spiritual center of a human being, so it is not a mere accident that the male genitals are inserted along this center into the female body. He explained this in detail. His explanation included concrete suggestions of sexual relationships. However, I will refrain from giving the details in this book.

The amount of spiritual energy flowing in the sexual center is in proportion to the radiance of the aura of a human body, and it gives off a silent message, he said. There are many kinds of Yahma to accomplish this, and when I practiced it a little bit, my head became clear and everything felt fresh. Since I came back to Japan, I have kept pouring the greatest energy into the practical study of this Yahma. Someday, I would like to report on it in detail, including the theory of the sexual center.

Once, Mr. M explained to me the relationships between the sexual center and the universe in very complicated Chinese. As far as I understand, it seems that the genital organ and the brain, which are located on opposite sides of the trunk of Tao, are something like electrodes where spiritual energy flows. In the same way every existence in the universe has this sort of energy of opposites, and sexual energy circulates within the great universe.

People in this village knew that all of the spiritual points of the human body are connected to the single sexual center, and activation of one of the spiritual points connects to activation of the sexual center itself. They attempted to improve bodily functions from this standpoint. Their understandings of the human body were reflected in every part of their culture, and their society seemed to be ultimately modeled on the structure of the human body, centered on its sacred axis. I will discuss this later.

Japanese would consider it strange to see a male and a female performing Yahma together, just as they would sexual intercourse. I have also seen groups of men and women doing Yahma together. About a week after I arrived in the village, I saw such a scene when I went into the forest. I met a couple, both were about 20, and the encounter destroyed all of my preconceptions about sexual relationships.

I came upon them suddenly as I walked, looking at the scenery in the distance. A naked female figure sat on a male lying on his back. I was puzzled more or less, however, I was not completely astonished because I had begun to understand their culture. She raised both of her hands above her head, the palms of her hands faced upward, and she hardly moved. It was clear from her face that she was in deep ecstasy in this prayer-like posture. She seemed not only still, but gave off the same still air as the man in the bamboo forest. It seemed to my eyes that something like intense electric current flew up her back, which bent slightly backward, and was transmitted through her hands up, and then emitted into heaven, far above. Her ecstatic praying posture changed gradually. She put her hands down, continuing to look diagonally upward, and kept this state for a fairly long time. She changed her posture into several other ones. Every posture as well as the movement of her body going from one posture to another were as beautiful as an elegant dance. It seemed that the female paid attention to her own sensations, changing her posture slowly as her inner energy wanted her to do. Her healthy tanned body seemed to shine in the sun, but more than that, it sparkled with the energy of her body. It is sometimes said that a halo appeared around a person's head. Her eyes, filled with supreme bliss, and her face, wrapped in indescribable love and warmth reminded me of creatures beyond humans, such as angels and Bosatsu. I was mesmerized by the space around her, which seemed to be filled with all things. The Tao, performed by these two people who seemed to have no desires at all, with huge tropical plants, Strelitzia, a bird of paradise, as background, could only be expressed as a great artistic activity involved with nature. Or it could be described as the ultimate religious dance expressing the Tao in the universe with their own bodies. Anyway, they were filled with overwhelming beauty and dignity. This artistic activity was in a completely different dimension from ours where we think that sexual desires are "despicable" and "shameful." It lasted for many hours, and I was not sure whether or not the man ejaculated in the end.

Why do human beings shine so divinely in sexual relationships? This couple could sympathize with each other's spirits and the wisdom of the natural world through their bodies, and follow the universe, which is equal to God in their concept. Their overwhelming brilliance embodied brilliance of wisdom in the natural world, as flowers shining in the field are the result of the embodiment of spirits in the natural world. It was the deepest art and the most modest prayer that a human being can express. I came to understand that ejaculation for ejaculation's sake, as perceived in civilized society and which I took for granted until then, was really narrow-minded. I noticed that we were possessed with the idea of sex as a self-centered act of desire. The sexual relationship should be a mirror that showed the person as he was, as is written in a Jewish sacred book. The figures of the couple were regarded as figures enhanced by love to become a god and goddess. I became aware of how humans have always faced their sexuality, and why it was God and Goddess for them. There was no reason to secretly perform so much sublime activity. It was natural to have an open sexual relationship for them!

First of all, we, civilized people, think that showing sexual activities to children is unwise from an educational point of view. However, it is because our sexuality is fulfilled in a particular dimension, is it not? The villagers perceived sexuality in a way completely opposite to ours. To them, sexual activity was exactly what children should be shown at an early age. Children were not taught that they themselves were conceived by way of shameful activities between their parents. On the contrary, they learned of figures of humans heading for divinity when they saw the holy Tao of the adults.

When abroad, I saw pious believers who prayed in a Catholic church. I was not a believer, but I was impressed by them as the unchanging shape of humanity. The figures of this couple in front of me in the forest had something in common with the Catholic believers. However, the beauty of a naked human being confronting divinity was more natural and beautiful than anything else I knew. Furthermore, I was astounded to find myself impressed by activities that had seemed before to be the opposite of pious human figures. This was a personal impression I had at that time; I realized there were two kinds of pleasant sensations in sexual relationships. One was the brain's excited condition caused by stimulating the genital organs which we generally experience. The other was a much deeper sensation of inflowing and circulating energy, something we cannot see. If I assume that there is a pendulum in our psyche, and it vibrates at a certain swing, the pleasant sensation of the sexual relationships we generally know is the condition in which the pendulum vibrates at the biggest swing; namely, it is caused by excitement as a trigger. On the other hand, it seemed that the pleasant sensation of the villagers was completely opposite, namely, it was caused by quieting the pendulum as much as possible, and therefore, it was a completely different kind of ecstasy. Because of this quiet condition in which participants did not allow vibrations, their bodies vibrated along the subtle waves in the world of nature, and reached boundless supreme bliss. I felt so. And because they considered it important, they would refrain from stimulating genital organs as much as possible. Besides, they were able to attain much deeper satisfaction from the latter, and they didn't have ideological sexual desires as we have, I imagined.

Regarding the term "sexual desires," I remembered that there was a sentence "無欲以觀其妙" in the 1st chapter of *the book of "Laozi."* This sentence means that we can observe the mysteriously profound pleasure the Tao brings through the sexual activities without sexual desires. Could it mean the condition of this quieted pendulum? The people in the village might have probed the truth of this sentence in their lives.

I saw their sexual relationships several times after that. Every time it was in mother nature. One of the reasons that they have sex in the beauty of nature might be similar to our own emphasis on mood. However, they differ from us in that they do not make much of mood, nor do they seek for anything but mutual sympathy and communication with the beauty of mother nature. I asked Mr. M about it, and he said:

"That is right. During the sexual activities, the spirit of a human being becomes like a blank sheet of paper which can be influenced by many things. That is why we choose a place filled with good aura. Of course, the word "good aura" is an expression of the Han race, and we don't have such expression. We put it in the words with the expression of meaning "a place where the spirits work actively."

Skin becomes extremely sensitive during sexual activities, as you know. It is so greatly heightened that a very subtle stimulus will cause more sensation than usual. The reason why people become innocent during sexual activities is that a deep concentration is produced naturally. This heightened sensation is easy to connect to the perception of a more exquisite wave, as it were, mutual sympathy with grand nature.

Human bodies are able to feel a pleasant sensation through physical stimuli. However, the dimension of pleasure which cannot be compared is the pleasure by mutual sympathy with grand nature. The human body, from head to foot, is, in a sense, a belt of sexual sensation where people communicate with grand nature. Yahma is also a way to heighten sensation.

This culture of Yahma began before the era of Laozi, so it is a matter of course that Laozi was brought up in such a culture. He was gifted with the power of grasping the truth intuitively through his heightened bodily sensation in that way. That is why he could describe the deep insight about sexuality."

According to Mr. M, it seemed that something like psychic trauma is decreased by half in a moment through activities such as Yahma, which included sex, even when they are not performed with such a purpose. Of course, they seem to have a great effect on the beauty of females.

Yahma is very effective for connecting with the Tao. However, it is not easy for civilized people to reach the complete 常道, the eternal Tao, because they are imprinted with various concepts, Mr. M said.

Any concept that isn't harmonious with the melody of grand nature becomes an obstacle to sexual energy. Mr. M called this obstacle "selfishness." The selfishness that Mr. M meant seemed something like a barricade which blocked the flow of sexual energy. The greatest experience I acquired in this village was that I could remove this barricade toward sexual energy. What I experienced was somehow like a great Yahma in a group. I would like to describe it in the last chapter.

Chapter 10

Dancing toward the Tao

—Toward the door through which the dimension ascends to a higher level!

A holy festival that leads to a feeling of oneness with all things.

I was in the sea of consciousness which was filled only with love.
What a happy feeling.
All of the negative feelings that I couldn't deal with,
such as the wounds
which I had experienced in my life until then
and the negative ideas and thoughts
which had been repressed,
were going to melt, I felt.

Festivals are performed almost every day in this village.

I was allowed to attend them. The place where they were performed was in the forest which was called "the forest of Gods."

This forest was located in the small mountains a short distance from the village. It had a feeling of grandeur—it was as if the gods lived there. When I was walking about 20 minutes from the village, I left the path and began walking into the mountains. I came to a round space, half covered thickly with the trees of the forest. Wherever I was in this village, I felt at ease, but when I was in this space, I felt especially safe and secure. My spirit felt tremendous yearning there.

A stone pillar stood in the middle of the small circle, and it felt like a house covered with trees. The stone pillar was about one meter high, and, when I looked at it carefully, I saw it was shaped like a phallus. It seemed very old and made me imagine an ancient ruin.

Mr. M explained to me that people had been performing festivals since ancient times in this place where the ancestor spirits dwelled and the Gods came from the heaven. I had a mysterious feeling when I imagined people several thousand years ago seeing this same scenery.

The people recognized that the space surrounding this stone pillar which towered vertically above us was a sacred space. They believed that the spirit came from heaven on to the central axis of this stone pillar, and then the space around it became a place where the spirit worked.

I was surprised to learn later that a phallic stone pillar which was very similar to this one in front of me was also found in Japan in some Jomon ruins. There is a theory that the totem poles of Indians and obelisks in Egypt were originally statues of vertically towering phalli. So, the pillar in Japan might have been based on the concept of a primitive sense of the cosmos, just as the pillars in this village were. In ancient Japan, the Gods were called "Hashira" which means "pillar." Modern people are unable to understand why the Gods were called pillars. This might have been the origin.

The festivals seemed to symbolize the meeting of the activities of the great spirits that transcended individual activities.

The villagers surrounded this stone pillar in a circle at the festival. Males and females took turns making the circle, and seemed to be greeting the pillar. The greeting was for the spirits, and also a prayer to them.

They believed that the ancestor spirits worked at the lower part of this stone pillar, and the celestial spirits at the upper part. However, each spirit was not individual, but part of all spirits together. Their concepts were different from ours on this point too. Anyway, in this way, they entrusted their consciousness to this stone pillar, which was the heart of all things.

I cannot forget the festival that I saw for the first time. The villagers faced the pillar which was the center of all, and stretched their arms forward with the palms of their hands facing heaven. The image of their divine figures at that time were burnt strongly into my mind. I remember that the atmosphere became hushed and still in a moment. It was like another world. It was as if the air itself came to a standstill. Only the swinging sound of the wind in the trees clearly reached my ears. When it was so still that even this could not be heard, the villagers brought their hands down slowly as if stroking their bodies. Watching, I felt the center of my body tremble. As they stroked their bodies, my own body sensed a mysterious feeling. It was as if I had experienced the same feeling a long time ago. They repeated the movements several times. I wondered if it had an effect on their minds, for I felt as if I were going into a different dimension. I had a feeling that both my body and soul were purified.

As long as it was not a special festival, the villagers began to dance immediately afterwards. This dance itself was the first part of the ritual.

There were big stones at four places outside each of the circles of people, and two or three men stand near the stones with rather big bamboo tubes in their hands. They played music for the dance. They beat the bamboo tubes together to make a tapping noise. The rhythm echoed from every direction, and sometimes the sound of beating the stone with the bamboo rang a different sound. There was also the sound of a drum made from a big trunk hollowed in the middle, and the unique utterances of the people. It was a world of sound and voice where the spirits mingled. I was impressed at the mysterious music these few elements created. It is really a pity that I cannot express the splendor of this music in words. Music is not what humans produce, but it is human behavior to recreate the rhythm that exists originally in nature. I was pulled into the unknown intoxication created by the energetic sounds and rhythm that echoed throughout the forest.

The circle of people turned around, stamping in a swinging rhythm to this music. They continued doing this until the entire circle made one revolution. It felt as though all of them had been unified into a single being. After one turn, they changed to another dance in which they raised and lowered their arms. Because they faced the center of the circle, they could see each other's expressions well. The frank and easy expressions of the girls on the other side of me induced me to feel indescribable yearning.

It was already evening and getting dark. Fire from the firewood behind the musicians and shadows of people cast by the fire gave rise to a unique atmosphere.

All of people danced concentrating on the stone pillar at the center. All of their consciousness centered on this one point. I felt as if my consciousness also melted into it, and I became one together with them. We kept dancing for about 30 minutes, I guess. Music became simple and the rhythm of 16 beats[21], and dancing became light and rhythmical. It reminded me of a jumping samba. The movement of all the people in a quick tempo, gave a pleasant feeling that my movement was a perfect fit to it, a pleasure that made me feel at one with the music, and with the space surrounded by power and heat. I was fascinated with them all. Then at a moment when I felt the spirits enhanced to a zenith which they had never before reached, the music stopped, people looked upward, and slowly raised their hands diagonally upward with the palms of their hands facing to heaven like a solemn prayer while continuing a sort of humming. At that time, I felt a deep stillness as if all things had stopped. In the stillness, the villagers turned the palms of their hands toward themselves three times, solemnly, as they received something from heaven. Then they took the hand of the person next to them, and the dancing stopped for a moment.

I felt a soft touch at the moment when I took the hands of the women on either side of me. The soft touch conveyed to me their entire psychic worlds. I cannot describe them in words. I felt, however, that

---

[21] It is a holy rhythm, which makes human souls resonate with the rhythm of the universe. For example, a gamelan and a kecak dance and chorus in Indonesia. There are many examples of 16 beats also in our daily lives.

they lived in psychic freedom, in a way completely different from us, and they received several phenomena through their sharp sensations, which were several times sharper than ours.

And I noticed that the sensation was connected to all of the people as they took each other's hands. It might be because I was influenced by the consciousness of people in this village that I was embraced by the feeling of oneness during this short stillness such as I had never experienced before. I had felt a feeling of oneness before, but this was on a level far beyond that.

It was clear that all of people had a deep feeling of oneness. Everybody had an expression on their face which could only be described as the best of art. They had an indescribable expression with which all things could be healed. A consciousness of such people was delivered not through my vision but through my body.

It was an experience of my consciousness that I had never had before.

Everybody was attractive. It didn't matter what their appearance was, but they had a similar outpouring of open happiness and merciful eyes as if they had embraced everything unconditionally. This peculiar atmosphere conveyed their supreme bliss in silence.

At the moment when I was surrounded by such joy, we began to dance as we held hands. The feeling of palpitation in their bodies made the females in front of me glisten more. It is not possible to describe my exalted feeling. Their bodies were polished to their limits by Yahma. They moved as naturally as fish in water. Their handmade clothes made them glisten, and their figures were just like celestial nymphs.

The exalted feeling this all produced was my own spiritual consciousness communicating with their spiritual consciousness (sexual energy) wasn't it? Was this not the pulsation of sexual energy?

The people were so beautiful and open, and their consciousness and my own consciousness intermingled in this feeling of oneness. It was beyond description, forcing me to change even my own self-recognition.

I felt different. I had never felt that I myself was such a wonderful and precious existence. I had not known who I was until then. When I looked around, all the men looked solemn and wise. Their eyes seemed to know all things, and they destroyed the images of human beings I had had until then. I was forced to notice that I had not seen anything of the people in this village nor this world until then.

I was in a sea of consciousness which was filled with only love. Everything in this space glittered as beautifully as the females did, and they were as solemn as they were lovely. It was as if this world in front of me changed in a moment. This feeling of ecstasy was, to be sure, far superior to the scope of sexual ecstasy.

The people made a circle together, and the dancing proceeded, turning slowly. We continued to hold hands. Then at every quarter rotation, an accented movement was performed. While the dancing was performed with this repetition, I became filled with a much deeper feeling of oneness with them. I felt as if all people were me. There was no wall between me and them, and I understood instinctively that they felt as I did. What a happy feeling. All the negative feelings that I couldn't deal with, such as wounds I had experienced in my life until then, and repressed negative ideas and thoughts, seemed to melt.

It was not a fleeting, temporary excitement. Since this experience my body has changed, and it senses this world differently from how it used to. It is difficult to describe what the difference is. However, the only thing that is clear is that I feel happy only from the fact that I am here. Since then I have come to know that happiness is not getting something. On the contrary, the notion of needing things to be happy is proof that one's life is far from happy.

(By the way, after I came back from this journey, my own personal problems were all resolved. It happened that things proceeded as miraculously as I had hoped. However, I think that the change in myself might have brought such results. I am describing all this as if it happened in a single day, but in fact I experienced them several times. However, each time the experience deepened, so I felt as if they happened only within a day.)

Every time I experienced this festival, my unconscious feeling of fear toward others strangely disappeared. For example, we have fears of others, in which we wonder what that person would think if we told them a certain thing, and therefore we build a wall. Such guardedness was removed through the deep feeling of becoming one. While I was a stranger in this village, this dancing in a group became a healing place for my psyche.

There was no communication with words. However, all things that I had sought were fulfilled in the silent communication.

This feeling became stronger every time I danced. Then on the day of a big festival, I happened to have the following shocking experience.

The usual festival was often performed by around a dozen people. However, almost all people gathered in this place for big festivals performed several times a year.

(The ancestral calendar in this village had 16^{22} months in a year. First of all, one year was divided precisely into four seasons, and each month into four weeks. Major festivals took place when the seasons changed. Besides this, there was a lunar calendar and they also performed moon festivals.)

A magnificent festival began with powerful music played by 20 or 30 people. The dancing began with the crowd of people sitting. It was really grand to see people move in the same way at the same time to the light rhythm of a 16 beat. I was wrapped in a great feeling of oneness in this atmosphere. My consciousness went into all people, and the minds of all people came into my consciousness.

The feeling of oneness was not only with people. I felt through my body that every blade of grass and each tree was alive. And not only grasses and trees, but the very movement of the air was also alive. All of the space of around me was alive. All of it was spiritual; I had

---

[22] Strangely enough, there are many important rhythms, cycles constructed in units of 16 in the universe. For example, the flower of the Japanese symbol (daisy) has 16 petals, as well as being a symbol in Sumer, and REM sleep and non-REM sleep cycles come every 90 minutes. This time correlates with the calculation, 24 hours / 16 = 1.5 hours.

the sensation that I existed in the sea of lives melting together in that place. All of existence was alive. I understood it not as a concept, but through my body. And the opposite was true, too. All of the countless existences in front of me were feeling my existence just as I felt theirs. I knew it not from my head, but from my body. Then this sensation of oneness produced something that filled me with satisfaction beyond description. This expression is not correct, but I cannot find a more appropriate one. The feeling of oneness with all things would be like this, would it not? My body felt such a fulfilled sensation that it was as if it was emitting electric shocks from the bones.

It was, to be sure, a kind of ecstasy. There is nothing that is close to this joy except sexual ecstasy, as Laozi says. However, sexual ecstasy is only a part of it. I realized that my ecstasy didn't stay only in my body, but spread into others. All things were my body, and the huge body was shaking with joy.

This experience made me notice various things.

I came to understand why old women in this village had such insights similar to divine possession. Communication among consciousnesses brings deep harmony and sympathy to people. The reason why the old women can see through anything must not have been only from the ability to observe things, but from the fact that they were in the dimension of consciousness that I was experiencing then. Actually, I was feeling what everybody felt and what their thoughts were, as if they were the sensation of my own limbs. I was sure if I were ordered to hurt someone, I would not do it, even to protect myself if I were in danger of being hurt. I felt such a deep love for everybody.

It was the heart of a human being, wasn't it? Up to now, I had thought of my heart as similar to a mere young bird inside an egg. What a world I discovered. All things were lovely. What a free liberating feeling! I myself spread to all.

I noticed that I was surrounded by people who grasped my hands tightly. They all knew what excitement I was wrapped in. Each person gazed at me with silent smiles as if they saw through my mind. I felt like an infant being carried in the bosom of a great mother who knew everything. I noticed that my eyes were filled with tears.

With the tears which wash away and purify all things, a barricade in my heart disappeared very naturally. The ego, which Mr. M calls pride, attachment, and hatred, which are barricades and impurities of the heart, disappeared from within me.

Suddenly, I realized that they had grown up in such a world. Children were among the people. They grew up experiencing what I miraculously finally felt at this age of my life. What a world it was!

Moral education in Japanese schools would not fit into even a single particle of the value of this experience. What we could learn here in this village was something much deeper than words; for example, saying we need to be thoughtful, kind, and cooperative. What we could learn here is so essential that we would not need any of these words at all.

Transcendence of worldly passions, spiritual enlightenment and so on, is discussed in the religions of civilized society. However, after this experience I couldn't help feeling that setting up the theme itself seemed too artificial and sounded prideful.

Their festivals were the best kind of morals, combining ideal physical training in which both body and spirit are stirred, along with music, which the whole body enjoys. In addition, it is the story of living history in which people learn the behaviors of ancient ancestors and the essence of wisdom. Furthermore, if we called the creation of harmony in society "politics," this festival could be called politics beyond description in which people are led to harmonious unity on the best level, even though there was no speaking at all. In fact, there were no politics in this village; this festival served to unite the whole village. Moreover, it was art in which people were brightened the most, and the brightened people themselves were the objects of art. Such beautiful and wholeheartedly made clothes, earthenware, and the village itself were all produced by these bright people. It is a system in which anything of education, politics, and art actualized something far beyond the ideal that civilized societies aim for. Besides it was a system in which only one activity accomplishes the ideal, and any activity was completed on a much more excellent level than civilized societies. What a culture it was!

All of the existences were filled and made alive by something like "oneness." A worldview similar to Laozi's must be the world that was expressed in this village.

昔之得一者，
天得一以精，
地得一以寧，
神得一以靈，
谷得一以盈，
萬物得一以生，
侯王得一以爲天下貞。
其到之一也。
(Chapter 39)

Once the eternal One is obtained,
heaven will become clear,
the earth will become stable,
the Gods will become divine,
the valleys will become overflowing,
all things will be born, and
kings will be the rulers of the world.
It is the One that lets these happen.

This was the world of Tao that Laozi meant!

In our civilized society, all education, politics, and art became more and more complicated. Then the essence is forgotten, hearts of children don't develop, and politicians think of only their own interests. Juvenile delinquency makes it seem as though young people have lost their humanity, shoplifting is a leisure activity of schoolchildren, and outrageous behavior at Coming of Age ceremonies by new "adults" appear to be anything but, and adults shamelessly pursue their own personal interests. These Japanese realities came to mind. What a difference it was in the village!

We have somehow come to believe that it is clever to become complicated. However, I was forced to realize that this notion was completely wrong. On the contrary, returning to oneness, namely, the wisdom of simplification was achieved to its ultimate level in this village. This is how highly efficient societies and energy-efficient societies are born. No time or physical material was wasted here.

I had always thought that human beings had to work, otherwise they could not earn a living. However, all of people in this village were exceptions. They used their time only for creative activities to improve themselves. They spent their everyday lives striving for what their own souls hoped for. This daily repetition brought straightforward kindness and brightness of humanity to them.

In the Japanese society where both of most couples work for a living, almost all of the day time is monopolized by work. I always thought it was the true state for all humanity. However, after I came to this village, I began to think about what a society was, what a state was on earth. Our society was only a slave society, where people were bound by the economy and paralyzed not to recognize slavery for what it was. Moreover, even religions that nurse our souls are bound by work to acquire believers in our society. Compared to this, even though they are not taught what they should believe at all in the world of this village, all children and adults revere what they should revere, and furthermore they look as if they themselves are celestial nymphs or wise men.

Probably in ancient times, such a society existed naturally. I reflected on how wrong my own images of ancient society were. I felt ashamed of the society I belonged to. It appeared too violent. Maybe in the ancient times of human beings, all societies were ideal, like in this village, however, once a society became greedy and sought to grasp power, it gradually brought the world to its present condition where everything is under the state's control.

Society, collectively, can be thought of as education, art, politics, physical training, leisure, religion, and more. At the same time, it is a means of information transfer, where thousand-year-old or ten-thousand-year-old wisdom of the ancestors may be conveyed, as well as being a history of culture, an elusive concept.

Now our civilized society has expanded its complications exponentially, like a sort of Big Bang, and, at its height, it is out of control. However, I felt that I was taught in this village how to make society simple again.

Readers may think that my description is exaggerated. However, I feel rather irritated with myself because I cannot express my excitement well enough. I have written many things, yet, what I would most like to convey is only one point: what the feeling of oneness was on earth.

Even though I try to convey it, my poor ability to describe hinders me. I don't know how to convey my experiences to people, which are several times deeper than my expressions. I am writing this book with a hope that you, the readers, will fill in the blanks of my inadequate expression with your imagination.

I had always felt somehow that human beings would try to get along with each other, but on the contrary, they criticize and deny each other, and there is no help for it. However, I experienced a condition where unconscious precautions or dreaded feelings toward others were not necessary at all, and what a happy condition that was.

It was as if I was in a sea of love consciousness. We each are only receivers of the consciousness which is like the sea, and we share the same consciousness. It is really impossible to express such an indescribable relief.

If I had recalled Japanese society while I was in this village, it would have seemed unreal. Compared to the reality of this village, I felt Japanese society was a vain imaginary illusion. And the society, where people hated each other and were forced to work as cogs in the gears of the system seemed a queer world, even though it was the society where I lived. I took for granted the obligation of children to go to school. However, once I saw the children in this village, I came to think that the Japanese society was guilty of taking away the free existence of children and binding them into the framework of compulsory education. The children in this village were brought up from birth to be loved by all the villagers. A mother is never forced to care for her baby all alone in a private room. Girls under the age of ten, especially, all loved babies. They were in the habit of asking mothers with babies to allow them to care for them for a while. It was the complete opposite of Japanese pupils who are pressed only to go to school and after-school tutoring. So, like the three girls whom I met at first, the eyes of children in this village made me feel intelligence that I never saw in the eyes of Japanese children. That gave me a great culture shock, because I had believed that the Japanese way of education was advanced. I was so shocked by the "intelligence" of the villagers that transcended knowledge. Young females in Japan are pressed to "work," namely, busily taking care of children. They say "children are troublesome" and so on. I feel such a term is terribly unsound. When I saw so many kind people filled with humanity in this village, I thought I understood the reason why even children in Japan hurt each other. As Laozi says, this world would be completely paradoxical. In Japan, where people use flowery words like "education," education is lacking. On the contrary, in this village where the word "education" didn't even exist, the most ideal education existed. What on earth had I believed so far!

In this village I came to wonder whether things we Japanese consider valuable were actually so. For example, we often say "let's do our best" or "please do your best." However, they don't live like we are doing our best, whereas the villagers led lives that appeared much more cordial and sincere toward people than in Japan. Besides, their way of life looked more genuinely creative than that of the Japanese. When I look at the Japanese from the point of view of the people in this village, the concept of the Japanese "doing our best" is an extremely aggressive concept. On reflection, in countries where people do their best, cruel wars are fought. Both the Germans, who do the best work of all Western countries, and the Japanese, who keep the largest number of people who die from overwork, are remembered in history for the most barbaric wars in the East and West. On the other hand, are there any peoples who caused a war without having the concept of doing their best? People on the southern islands, who have no such concept at all, have not caused any wars, of course, and even the Indians, some of whom try to do their best, have not produced any wars. Countries that cause wars are, without exception, those which place importance on labor for profit. Environmental destruction is also always in direct proportion to the degree to which a society emphasizes doing one's best.

When I was surrounded by the villagers, it felt as though I had found the true peaceful way of human beings. People in this village had a way of life which was beyond the dimensions of both doing one's best and the opposite of it.

Now Asian countries are in the biggest crisis we have ever experienced. Folk cultures, which have been cultivated over thousands of years, are being suddenly swallowed by an advancing wave of civilized economy. These ancient cultures are destroyed in a moment. This is happening everywhere. A big gulf between rich and poor is created, and people who are driven into lower classes are unable to earn a living. Worlds of robbery and falsehood are produced. Such a social change transforms the quality and structure of human relations which had been harmonious before. It even undermines the bond of family. Society overflows with people who have lost their homes. What happened gradually in Japan over a hundred years, now we see within a short period: changes attacking people, which is a rather crushing phenomena.

Now, people in Asia have begun to reflect on what we have lost. They have objectively begun to realize the value of their own culture. However, they have difficulty in understanding what the cultural root is, the thing that has supported their hearts. Moreover, they have lost their way back. I had this experience many years ago, and it was still before the time when many parts of Asia were involved in such situations.

Through this experience, I might have met the common cultural root of various Asian peoples.

Chapter 11

Filled with Love (the great Tao)

—The social system like the natural world.

> *All desires are born to compensate for unattainable love.*
> *Where true love exists, there is no desire.*
> *And true love does not ever arise*
> *without experiencing the great Tao*
> *which is sacred, transcending personal sexuality.*

Later, I learned the following. When people are given some existence from the natural world to maintain their lives, they pray for them, as in the culture of the Ainu.[23] The prayer looks like a song and also a dance for our eyes. The people purify the place with their voices, make the space breathe with their dancing, and they are bound directly with the gods.

When I learned this, I thought this rang true in my experiences. Come to think of it, also in Western folk dances, people make a circle, hand in hand, for example in "Mayim Mayim," and dance in a similar way to this dance. I don't know if Mayim Mayim has such a long history, however, folk dances themselves may be based in a root, basal culture of human beings. Long ago, Oriental and European basal culture may have been connected.

---

[23] The Ainu are indigenous inhabitants across Japan and the northern part of Russia.

The beginnings of activities of human beings, namely dancing like this, might conceal all of the powers that human beings seek.

There are two obvious changes which happened to me after that experience.

One was that I became wrapped in a kind of ecstasy every time I went into the forest. I came to feel that a great interchange occurred between the trees and the flowers in the forest. I came to realize the activities of spirits that the girls in the village honored, not as a concept but through my body. For the first time I could understand the deep ecstatic feelings people had when they were performing Yahma alone in the forest.

I came to receive inspirations more and more, and as a result, sometimes I am even able to foresee the issues by hunch, such as life's events as well as global truths.

I was brought up in Japanese society, and had believed that males and females were to love each other on the one hand, and hate each other on the other. I saw many entanglements of relationships between males and females, and watched dramas on TV. I internalized the idea that they were normal people. However, as I lived in this village, my concept about human beings was quickly destroyed. I never saw even a single entanglement between male and female in this village. Far from that, I never saw even a trivial dispute between males and females of the sort so common in Japan. In the village, they were brought up wrapped in the love that I experienced in the festival, so they were never hungry for love or sought for love. They never tried to force anyone to love them. On the contrary, everybody tried to give love to the others as a matter of course. This satisfaction with love naturally created the ideal relationship between males and females.

After the experience in that village, I came to understand how hungry Japanese people were for love. People in the village didn't aim for the opposite sex with a personal intention, such as to possess the opposite sex as its own, to confess its own need to be understood and so on. As I experienced at the festival, their consciousness connected with each other in this village. The feeling of love was different from ours; it came out of their sympathy for each other. Therefore, they knew that when one loved another person, that person loved them too. Then when a person felt love toward another, it was natural that it was already conveyed to the other without having to express it verbally. I never saw anyone who suffered from one-sided love as people in the civilized societies do.

They find the right person on a dimension of which we are unable to see. So, it would be natural for them to look filled with happiness. When I saw them, I realized that human beings are fated to meet their perfect match in the opposite sex from the start. The story of "the romantic thread of fate" is told as if it is just a dream in Japan, yet, it is a normal reality in this village. So, they married early to a favorite partner at 14 or 15 years of age. When I saw them, I felt that marrying at this age was natural.

They didn't have any concepts to bind their partner by possessive desire or jealousy, so they maintained a harmonious and intimate relationship with the other members of the opposite sex even after marriage. Moreover, they didn't even have any controlled marriage patterns as we have. Their marital lives were not controlled by laws or government. According to the conditions, there seemed to be many patterns of marriage, such as one husband with some wives, one woman with some men, a night-visitation marriage, and so on, all based on one husband with one wife. To my surprise, even though several patterns of marriage existed freely, a perfect balance was kept as a whole. The whole of the relationship between males and females in this village created such a perfect harmony, as if all were united into one complicated organic existence. The reason for this might be, as expected, that the consciousness of all the villagers was bound with the center of the oneness. It even seemed that they were bound with all of the opposite sex in the village through the feeling of oneness, which is deeper than that of ours toward our wife or husband. Their daily lives were filled with physical contact. It was as if all people were lovers who understood each other, and no jealousy was felt because of physical contact with the opposite sex. It was because they didn't have a personal desire to seek for the opposite sex within their psyche, where they are satisfied with the great Tao. The fact that they didn't have possessive desire toward the opposite sex must have built such a free oneness as a result. It was the same toward other living beings. It was impossible to monopolize a fortune, and they didn't have a concept of a fortune itself.

Behind all of their loves were not only the love between males and females, but the great love (great Tao) which includes all things. And their festival was the very thing that sustained the great love!

Civilized people have lost the great Tao, which is the essence of this love. That is the reason why they cannot obtain love even though they seek it.

After that experience, I came to marvelously understand the mental state in which people are so hungry for money or power.

The desire by civilized people for tangible things is a compensation for lack of love. We have confused the spiritual world and the material world in our psyches. A mental state in which a person has the illusion of getting love from the opposite sex, produces the illusion of getting love also from material goods. Such a mental state is conceived from the fact that people feel satisfied by shopping in a department store. In civilized society, people have developed a desire for possessions, which is in fact a perverted desire for love. Modern capitalism is the system that sprang up at a saturation point of such a perverted desire for love.

When the psyche is not satisfied with love, it produces a desire for power as well. When the psyche has the illusion that it can possess love by making others its own, it feels pleasure from making many people its own by controlling them. The subconscious has an illusion that it is acquiring love. This perverted desire for love is the peculiar desire of civilized people, which is called desire for power. If you observe them well, it is clear that the more a person is full of desire for power, the more he or she has past experiences of not being satisfied with love. In this way, countless desires are confronted with each other and fights give rise to other fights.

All the tragedies of civilized societies, such as hatred, destruction, fights, loneliness, unsound psyche, are caused by only one loss. It is the loss of true love. They are the tragedies caused by one loss, which should be at the center of a human being.

People in this village didn't have any desires at all for power nor material goods as we have. This meant there were no tragedies in this society as we have in ours. It was because they were satisfied with true love from the beginning. It was because they had not lost the one point that was the central point of human beings.

All desires are born as compensation for unattainable love. Where true love exists, there is no desire. And true love does not ever arise without experiencing the great Tao, which is sacred, transcending personal sexuality. I learned this at that festival in the village, where the way of original existence of human beings has been miraculously maintained. I think that experience was also an initiation for me. I, an unsound civilized person, could return to my natural humanity.

When I reflect, all the problems that modern civilization faces would be solved if this "desire" was cleared. The problems of environment, which would not be difficult to solve if human beings were united harmoniously, the problems of war, and the problems of desolation of the spirit, all of them are produced from this abnormal desire for love. I am sure that the experiences which I had in this village contained the way to solve the big problems in modern society all at once.

The entire abnormal psyche is produced from the distortion of love. The abnormal psyche is not exclusive only to criminals; it is the common psyche for all people in civilized society. Since my experience, I realized that even many of the very usual feelings, which Japanese didn't think of as abnormal at all, were based on the perverted desire for love. The distorted psyche of desire for love lurks behind the usual feelings such as jealousy, a competitive spirit, a sense of superiority, or even a sense of justice. Many fights of the civilized people are produced from this unsound sense of justice. The psyche in which people can feel happiness only from hurting somebody is a stereotype of unsound psyche of civilized people. I recognized how unsound the feelings which I had overlooked so far were. Such a cognitive faculty was born in me unnoticed.

Mr. M said, "Love arises from love, and appreciation arises from appreciation." Or when he talked about people living in cities, he said, "Discontent causes discontent, and hatred causes hatred." I began to understand without any explanation what kind of psychic structure or activity creates such conditions.

Where recognition exists, no tragedies are born. Because civilized people cannot even recognize such psychology, they don't have an awareness of the problems involved at all. It is a big difference between us and people in the village.

In such an expansion of recognition, where something not to be seen is seen, people would have called "satori" (spiritual enlightenment). However, this word also came to be used to show power of a religious person in the religious world, and "satori" became something special for special people. The essential figure of human beings without such authorization exists in this village.

It is often said that only human beings among all of the animals in our environment destroy nature, claim the lives of others unnecessarily, and have impertinent ideas. However, people in this village showed that the ways of life in our society are wrong. Among all creatures, they valued their lives the most and harmonized with nature on the highest level as human beings. And above all, their existence radiates most brilliantly.

What else can this be, except progress as human beings? Rather, more than the progress as human beings, they have achieved proper evolution. It is the appropriate evolution for the lord of all creation.

Civilization directed our attention only to the outer world, and we believed that improvement meant progress. However, a society that considers progress as improvement becomes a society with increased complications. For example, the bosom of a family was lost when TV was introduced; people became addicted to TV, so they needed something in compensation for what was lost. With the increased number of cars, the air became polluted, traffic accidents increased, the legs and backs of people became weak, so they also needed something in compensation for them. Our concept of progress for human beings, such as having TVs and cars, only valued the outer development, which always made things complicated. Then, on such a basis, we have looked down on the village's culture as an undeveloped culture, and absorbed a sense of superiority. And we have forgotten to proceed forward, not even noticing what we have forgotten, as the rabbit in the story "The Hare and the Tortoise."[24]

On the contrary, people in this village have steadily evolved as humans, which is the most important thing, and developed it so far that we can't reach them.

The truth is that they were very developed people who were so far ahead of us. I am sure of this.

The reason why they made such progress must be that the culture of the transcendental experiences has been kept, only by which all can be overcome and all can be cultivated.

This village could be described as a society which has progressed most properly on earth by the world of "oneness" that Laozi mentioned.

---

[24] This is a famous story from Aesop's Fables. A hare made fun of a tortoise because the latter moves very slowly. But the tortoise said that he would win if they did a race. So, they decided to compete. The hare, confident of winning the race, took a nap on the way. The tortoise kept walking forward slowly, and finally reached the goal before the hare.

Chapter 12

The Code of Laozi which was unsealed

—The reason why Laozi concealed it.

For modern religions, paying attention to sexuality is under-stood as only a "sinful desire." However, the same thing was regarded as mentality, which was the nearest to the gods.

There are various folks and various cultures in the world. However, if we trace the history, the common culture of human beings appeared at a certain era. It is a culture that was named animism by scholars in which they recognize the divinity within all things.

It is said that genital worship prevailed widely in an era of the universal culture for human beings. There are shrines and temples as the religious places in our time, but if we go back to more than a certain era, they disappear. Instead, statues of male genital organs or female ones were placed at the center of the holy place. They are the only statues, which are shaped like genitals, and the people respected, through them, that "sexuality" itself was the center of all things.

For modern religions, paying attention to sexuality is understood as only a "sinful desire." However, the same thing was regarded as mentality, which was the nearest to the gods. What does the contrast tell us? Namely, the contrast between the modern religions that regard sexuality as going astray, and the ancient concept of the universe, which is worldly universal, with sexuality regarded as an entrance toward the gods.

Modern people keep out sexuality, but they inflate their desires, and they have produced a sexual culture as an outlet for their desires. We have reached an age where sexuality is kept out externally, but tempts people like a devil as a culture of huge desires behind it.

In ancient times, people did not have a double standard for sexuality. Sexuality was always the central point for them. Sensation of the human being and magnanimity are born from there, furthermore, a route of sensation that we don't know is born from there. They would have known them, wouldn't they?

I have not studied Leonard da Vinci[25] in depth. However, it is said that Mary of Magdalene is painted to look like John standing next to Jesus in his painting "The Last Supper."[26] The technique of painting the apparent contents and the "hidden" essential contents doubly is similar to the technique with which Laozi wrote *the book of "Laozi."*

Concerning the painting of da Vinci such as "The Madonna of the Rocks,"[27] two paintings are painted with identical structures. It is said that his ideological insistence is drawn in code in one of them.

Laozi had double meanings for one sentence. One meaning was out of the question from the ordinary point of view in the world, and

---

[25] It seemed that Leonard da Vinci was a grand master of the priory of Sion. The priory of Sion is a secret society which has a history of several thousand years. Its essential purpose is not clear, but it is said that its purpose is to protect the sacred line of children born between Jesus and Mary of Magdalene. So, it is thought that da Vinci concealed sacred symbols within his paintings to give clues to deeper meanings than the subjects themselves.

[26] "Mary of Magdalene" was a woman who came from Magdalene, and was one of the disciples of Jesus. It is said that she was very close to Jesus, not only as a disciple, and it is even said that she was his most beloved. There is also a theory that she was his partner or spouse, and gave birth to his daughter named Sarah. It is not clear if this theory can be understood only symbolically, or is based on fact. However, it has something to do with liberation from the suppression of females, femininity, and sexuality.

[27] This painting was ordered by a religious organization to show one part of legends of orthodox Christianity, which is a coincidental meeting of John the Baptist and an angel, Gabriel. The Holy Mother is in the middle of two sainted children, and one of her left side is accompanied by the angel Gabriel, who was given a mission to protect John the Baptist. Da Vinci didn't mention which child was Jesus or John. But in his paintings, Jesus who was considered to be on the right side of the Holy Mother, John on the left side, so the organization didn't accept it, because the painting meant that John was under the protection of the angel much more than Jesus. Then the second version was ordered. In the second one, John is on the right side of Mary and holding a cross which gives an association of John as being accepted by the organization. There are more differences between the two paintings, but I refrain from mentioning them to stay with the book.

the other was difficult to be accepted. The completely same poem is written as the contents he insists on one hand, and as a camouflage to be accepted in the world on the other hand.

It is similar to the technique of da Vinci who painted "The Madonna of the Rocks," with one meaning accepted in Christian society as a camouflage for another meaning that could not be accepted. Moreover, the ideological contents themselves, which are expressed with such a technique, are also similar to each other.

The common point is, needless to say, "sexuality." The society in which Leonard da Vinci lived was Christian. People in the world believed all things according to the Church's doctrine. Compared with it, the contents that he insisted through his paintings included disposition that could destroy such an existent authority. Because of the negative values of sexuality, they needed to draw the image of Jesus as if he had not had any sexual relationships, as Jesus was born without any sexual relationships.

However, da Vinci would have seen through the foolishness of this thought as well. So, he would have tried to point it out in code through the painting.

It is the same as with Laozi. The society where he lived was the Chinese society where Confucian ideas were becoming the authoritative thought in the world. As da Vinci spread his own thoughts by concealing them under his paintings in case they were crossed out by the authority of the Church, Laozi concealed his own thoughts under his poetries in case they were crossed out by the authority of Confucianism in such society. More than 2,000 years before Leonard da Vinci was born, Laozi left his messages to posterity with the same technique.

What da Vinci insisted was approval of sexuality. He thought that sexuality didn't draw people from God at all, and he put his idea into his paintings in a society where they denied sexuality. Laozi is the same. Or rather his insistence was much deeper than da Vinci. The center of his insistence does not turn our eyes away from sexuality, but makes us look at it deeply, and moreover we attempt to recover humanity by mastering the truth of it.

Da Vinci and Laozi. They were pioneers who sowed seeds so that they could sprout to be brought back to life when the right time came; seeds, namely, of the natural figures of human beings, their beauty, and nobility which were crossed out by the authorities.

They sowed the seeds secretly so as not to let the world know about it prematurely.

Unfortunately, this sexuality which should be the most precious for life has become an object to be despised the most in civilized religions. Sexuality was looked down on as if it were vulgar to talk about it.

Laozi is the first thinker who tried to revive the original recognition of sexuality into civilized society. Every thought in civilized society is made up of words, and it is absolute virtue when it is in print. In such a situation, the original religious recognition of sexuality without text was expelled entirely as vice. Laozi was the person, who tried to revive this original religious recognition of sexuality beyond writing, intentionally using words as signals.

However, this fact was sealed and nobody learned of it. He described it with excellent code so thinkers in the civilized society would not see through it easily. After that, his thoughts were sealed completely on a universal scale. 2,500 years passed without the seal being broken by anybody.

As all things are composed of Yin and Yang, the principle of Yin and Yang work on the whole of human beings. What happens in the East can happen in the West, and the opposite is also the truth.

Da Vinci is the Western version of Laozi. And Laozi is the Eastern da Vinci. The time to break the seal of Laozi might have come, just as da Vinci was decoded.

Chapter 13

Time to say goodbye

—Ecstasy of life and spirit, being embraced by the boundless supreme bliss.

In the entirely same manner as their bodies were open,
The hearts of the girls were completely open toward human beings.
How can I express this peculiar sense
in which I shared the feeling of "oneness" with such girls?
I cannot find the right word to properly describe this feeling
of happiness.

Well, in this way I learned the secret of *the book of "Laozi"* through my accidental meeting with Mr. M. I have been busy, so I have not visited that village again since I came back to Japan.

People in that village were very, very warm to me from the beginning, and especially since my experiences at the festival, I was completely connected with them with the feeling of "oneness." On the day when my journey was going to be over, five girls, including Mendla, whom I met at first, invited me for bathing.

It was not far from the village to the river. We walked toward the river along the peaceful and narrow path.

When we arrived at the river, they took off their clothes, went into it and beckoned me in. I also became naked and went into the river. The water was comfortably cold and pure. They made merry diving and swimming in the clean and transparent water. I was also swimming and making merry with them without my realizing it. There was no wall between us at all; it was as if our naked figures symbolized the world of our psyche.

I noticed that I was satisfied with the feeling of freedom in my heart much more than in my body at that time. In Japanese society, all people have something that they don't want others to know at the center of their hearts. However, the girls in the village must have had no secrets at all. In the entirely same manner as their bodies were open, the hearts of the girls were completely open toward human beings. How can I express this peculiar sense in which I shared the feeling of "oneness" with such girls? I cannot find the right word to properly describe this feeling of happiness.

After a while, they began to sing a song. It was not a song which Japanese can imagine. It was like the peal of spirits that spurted from their whole bodies. Their comfortable voices like humming, were boundlessly transparent, resounding around there, and solemn. They raised their hands over their eyes slowly like scooping up water to the sound like humming, and kept singing. When waters were gone, they brought their hands down turning the palm of their hands toward themselves, and scooped up water once again. I heard that it was a prayer of thanksgiving for the water god, however, before I was taught about it in words, I knew it because their modest behavior toward the august object showed it. The elegant movement of their hands was connected with that of their waist, and the line from the tips of their fingers to their waists moved gracefully, like they were flowing. The brilliant beauty of their wet long hair, their voices which echoed in the great nature; it was the purest thing I could ever experience.

Nothing is more beautiful than the beauty of spirits. I cannot help thinking so. This inspiring feeing was the emotion which cannot occur only from the mere visual beauty of their spirits. I found that I touched the purity of their spirits.

Because they knew very deep happiness, the pleasure came out from their bodies naturally. They gave pleasure from the natural world back to it, and tried to pleasure it at the same time. In reality, the air around them and the great nature resounded brilliantly with their dancing and voices. We don't know any styles to express our gratitude except expressing thanks in words. However, I felt as if I saw the essential human figures of gratitude inside of them.

Water is the most important spirit for females, they say. I felt ashamed that I had recognized water only as a form of matter until then.

I felt the feeling of "oneness" with this comfortable and cold water. Water was vividly alive. I felt mysteriously comfortable about my skin touching such water. Not only water, but the air around me which brought a refreshing breeze was continuously alive. The birds singing also reached my ears not as mere sounds but as songs which brought pleasure. I felt that the mountains spread widely at a distance were also one of the figures of my soul.

Every time I had natural eye contact with one of these innocent girls, I felt that this sensation was many times greater than I felt in nature when I was alone. They were younger than me, however, I felt in their eyes that they were much more broad-minded than anybody I met in Japan. That would be because this sensation in them was much stronger than in me. It would be easy to describe it as "kindness" in a single word. I met more extraordinary great "kindnesses" than I had never known before. My soul was satisfied with the communication with the girls beyond our bodies; it was as if I was given all things I sought. Why did Laozi express "sexuality" and "the essential way of life" in a single word? I understood the meaning of it very well now.

I felt as if a fairly long time had passed. One of them made her way to the beach from the river.

She walked on the sand, step by step. Her long wet legs were tanned much more healthily than mine, and shining. I loved the sight of their naked backs walking in nature, and it made me feel a yearning for home.

After we all came out of the river to the river side and took a rest, the youngest, Mendla, gave me a bag which she had carried on her shoulder on her way there. I knew from her shy smile that it was a present for me. I opened it. There were the clothes that they would have woven from the depths of their hearts and a loincloth made of leaves of the same tree as theirs.

They came to the river for bathing with this natural skirt more often than with the clothing made of cloth. It was because they thought nothing of getting wet in the skirt.

I imagined that they knew that the time to say good-bye would be close, so they would have woven into the clothing their prayers for me to be protected by the spirits of the tree.

I put them on, and walked back with them.

When I look back, I had never worn the same clothes as the people in this village, so it was the first time to do so. It was a marvelous pleasure for me that we wore the same clothing. I felt that I could go back to the natural state of a human being for the first time of my life. I felt that I was accepted as one of the people in this village.

I was filled with boundless supreme bliss only by the fact that I was walking on the same path wearing the same clothes as the girls.

Selections from *the Book of "Laozi"*

The book of "Laozi" is originally written so that one sentence is understood in double meanings: as Yin and Yang. The combination of Yin (secret meaning) and Yang (public meaning) describe the essential meanings that Laozi wanted to express.

1. The ultimate Tao

道可道非常道, 名可名非常名。
無名天地之始, 有名萬物之母。
故常無欲以觀其妙, 常有欲以觀其徼。
此兩者, 同出而異名。
同謂之玄, 玄之又玄, 衆妙之門。 (Chapter 1)

Secret (Yin) meaning

I will tell you about a secret of sexuality.

However,

I would not like to talk about changeable sexual relationship,

the type you often experience.

Ultimate sexuality is unnamed essence,

one that has given birth to this universe.

The sexual relationship that you know

is only the pseudo-expression of its true nature.

Thus, we should see the true nature of sexuality,

beyond the physical passionate dimension.

Beyond the joy of wild sex you know,

a world of supreme bliss is in its depths.

If you feel an attraction toward merely temporal sexual relationships,

then why don't you try to understand the much deeper world which is concealed underneath?

This world is the ultimate sexuality, namely,

the sphere of supreme bliss,

something far beyond everything in the universe.

This is what I would like tell you about-the way to ultimate ecstasy, namely love.

119

Public (Yang) meaning

The Tao that can be expressed by words
is not the absolute Tao.
The Name that can be named
is not the absolute Name.
However, each existence,
was born from the named existence
that was created from the nameless movements.
Therefore, when you become free of avarice,
you come to see the mysterious movements.
You see only the superficial world opposing it
as long as you have avarice.
Both the named sphere and the nameless sphere
come from the same source,
with the difference named or nameless.
The deepest movements behind these very profound
movements create everything.

Meaning of both sides combined

The Tao which can be described in words as the true Tao,
is not the unchangeable absolute truth at all.
Something truly unchangeable
cannot be understood within these words.
However, there is a moment when anybody can catch a
glimpse of the true Tao.
It is a sexual sensation through the body,
positioned in the opposite to the tip of the head.
However, it is also only a model of the true Tao.
The Tao you know (sexual relationships and the ecstasy
following it)
is only an imitative expressions of the true Tao.
The unchangeable activity of the universe
concealed in the far depths of it is the true Tao.
Therefore, you see, the essence of this universe
is the ultimate ecstasy.

2. Guide of all

孔德之容, 惟道是從。
道之爲物, 惟恍惟惚。
惚兮恍兮, 其中有象。
恍兮惚兮, 其中有物。
窈兮冥兮, 其中有精。
其精甚眞, 其中有信。
自古及今, 其名不去, 以閱衆甫。
吾何以知衆甫之狀哉。以此。

(Chapter 21)

Secret (Yin) meaning

The vessel (容) of the hole (孔) of the female genital organ (德)
follows the pokes of the male genital organ (道).
When the male genital organ pokes,
the female genital organ falls into ecstasy
and leaves all things to take their own course.
When the male genital organ emits sperm (精),
the female genital organ just accepts them in ecstasy.
In the very ecstasy,
sperm is emitted
into the deep and mysterious hole (窈兮冥兮).
I see the highest truth
in the depth of this sexual phenomenon,
which is undeniably creative.
The essence of the immutable heaven is there.
The essence is beyond time,
and it is also the power to rule over all things.
The reason
why I understand all the rules
is that I observe all things
in the depth of this sexual activity.

Public (Yang) meaning

Figures of people of the great Tao
just follow the truth of origin.
The Tao creates a clear world
from the vague and faint dimension.
In the very great depth,
mysterious activities take place.
The energy is extremely real,
and holds the truth inside itself.
From the past to the present,
its name is never lost.
It is the existence as a wise old man,
who watches over the beginning of all.
The reason why I understand all the rules
is due to the Tao.

Meaning of both sides combined

A man of real virtue is a man who surrenders himself to
the teaching of the Tao.
He becomes like a woman
who surrenders herself to her man.
As the woman is implanted with sperm
in a pleasant feeling of ecstasy,
a person in the supreme bliss
is shaken by the essential wisdom (精) in the universe
and trembles with its pleasure.
As a small spermatozoon builds the human body without
a mistake,
The invisible wisdom (精)
leads all things as they should be.
This wisdom (精) is the very eternal and unchangeable
essence,
which is beyond all of the phenomena.
The reason why I understand all the rules
is due to this holy spirit (精),
which is beyond the sexual energy (精).

3. Union of Heaven and Earth
天門開闔, 能爲雌乎。
明白四達, 能無知乎。
生之畜之, 生而不有。
爲而不恃, 長而不宰。
是謂玄德。
(Chapter 10)

Secret (Yin) meaning
Look at a woman who reaches ecstasy,
with her genital organ opening and closing.
Her whole body is filled with the supreme bliss
and she becomes one with the world of every direction,
and feels and masters all things,
however, she is an existence of being free from anything.
A life is born in such a condition.
She, who is unified with heaven and earth,
brings up her child warmly,
but does not possess it.
Whatever she does well,
she doesn't boast of it,
nor is she proud that she is loved.
The very figure of such a woman is the mystic woman,
namely, "the profound female 玄德."

Public (Yang) meaning
Control the invisible gate in yourself
which receives guidance from heaven
as the feminine who can manipulate the gate.
Awake your consciousness
and behave like a fool
with all your intelligence.
She who can do such things
doesn't possess her children,

even if she gave birth to them and raised them.
She doesn't boast of her great deeds.
She has no intention to control others,
even if she is in a certain position.
I call this "玄德," namely,
"the very profound existence of someone
who has mastered the Tao."

Meaning of both sides

The condition connected with heaven
is boundlessly close to a woman
in sexual relationship.
Thus, release your mind
as the woman who is embraced does.
Then you can reach the dimension
in which you become aware of all,
and knowledge is unimportant.
A person, who reaches such a holiness,
brings up all things without selfishness.
She thinks even of her own child
as not belonging to her.
(That is how a broad-minded child who is connected
with heaven is brought up.)
Whatever great things she does,
she has no intention of being proud of it.
Because she knows that all things are led by heaven.
(That is why she is in harmony and loved modestly.)
Even if she has a certain status,
she has no intention of controlling others.
(That is why she gives true happiness to people.)
"玄德" that I insist is
the dimension of supreme bliss
where people entrust all things to heaven
as a woman does her body to a man.

4. Sexuality without any form

反者道之動，
弱者道之用。
天下萬物生於有，
有生於無 。

(Chapter 40)

Secret (Yin) meaning

All things are created
by reciprocal action of its opposite,
such as an active activity (Yang),
like a male genital organ
bent backwards strongly, on the one hand,
and a passive activity (Yin),
like a female genital organ
accepting it softly, on the other hand.
Not limited to the human beings and life,
all things in this world are produced
by reciprocal action (an object's activity to produce
another object) like this.
And the essence,
which produces such reciprocal action,
is the very great Tao,
which surpasses relativity.

Public (Yang) meaning

Going back to your resource.
It is the nature of Tao,
even though its function is felt as weakness.
All things in the world
are born from existence with forms.
And, existence with forms
are born from existence without forms.

Meaning of both sides combined
Like sexual intercourse with a male organ
which is hard and active,
and a female organ which is soft and receptive,
all of existence is produced by the opposite operations
of Yin and Yang.
That which holds these opposite operations
of the source of all things,
is sacredness beyond existences.
The union with sacredness brings people back to their
origin.
It leads people to the dimension
where they don't fight with anybody
and it is beyond existence.

5. From Ecstasy to the Union

塞其兌, 閉其門, 終身不動。
開其兌, 済其事, 終身不救。
見小曰明, 守柔曰強。
用其光, 復帰其明, 無遺身殃。
是謂習常。
(Chapter 52)

Secret (Yin) meaning

If you keep your genital hole closed,
reach to the dimension
where you don't have to seek for it,
then you know a world
where there is no suffering.
If you open your genital hole
and only seek the pleasure of physical sexuality,
then you come to an end
without knowing the world of great love,
which is true supreme bliss.
Eyes which can see
the subtle Tao behind the phenomenon
are conscious minds,
and a person with such eyes
has flexibility of the soul
to live in the dimension of the Tao,
and has true absolute strength
which cannot be broken.
Anybody who comes back to this dimension
with the light of the Tao,
then can live in a world
where nobody is hurt.
It is what that I call "習常 learning the Tao."

Public (Yang) meaning
If you keep your sensuous holes opened,
and keep seeking for stimulus from outside,
then no wonder that you lose yourself.
Shut up the holes,
then you will not be exhausted.
Look in your inner world,
which is subtle within yourself,
not like the outer world.
Then you will understand the world
filled with soft and great love.
And you will become strong
filled with softness and weakness.
Feel the light within yourself,
go deep into it,
then you will be protected without being hurt.
This way of life is called "習常 learning the Tao."

Meaning of both sides combined
Try to close your genital hole.
Try to reach a dimension
where you don't have to seek for any desire.
Then, there is a free world
where you won't ever ruin yourself.
People in this world are like slaves of desire.
Because they don't know the true great love,
all they can do is to seek temporary love.
Look at the dimension of the Tao
behind this universe!
Go back to the absolute dimension
where you are free of change!
A light from this absolute dimension
leads people to the truth
that cannot be betrayed by anybody.
It is what I call "習常,"
namely, to enter the eternal world.

picture 1; Genital Statue worshiped in a miniature temple (Private collection of Amano family)

Beliefs of each family were prevalent all over Japan before civilization and enlightenment. But Japanese in this age don't know about it. The origin of these practices is much older than the introduction of Buddhism into Japan, the traditional polytheistic religion of Japan, or Shinto, based on which are government-organized shrines. However, this precious worldly historical culture was regarded as a barbarous custom, prohibited by the Meiji government, and then disappeared.

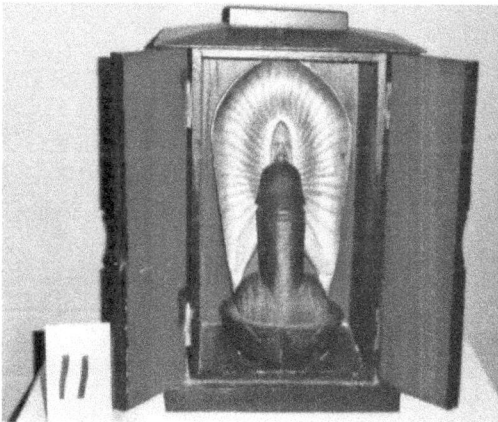

picture 2; Genital Statue worshiped in a miniature temple (Private collection of Amano family)

This was not a waggish custom for entertainment nor a special belief. It showed the inheritance of the most universal sacred concept of human beings, and was the most general culture of spirituality in Japan. Human beings respected the most sacred universe of sexuality from time immemorial.

129

Translator's Note

How do you feel after reading this book?

What thoughts are going through your mind?

You might have felt inspired or healed; or perhaps you experienced numinosity, or felt as if you were embraced by the universe. On the other hand, some might have questions about where the village is, and if the author really visited the village; was there actually such a village, or was this story from a vision or the author's imagination, like a fairy tale? Honestly, these points are not clear, but even so, that doesn't devalue the book's message. Perhaps that is why so many people have felt inspired and healed by this story. Even if I boldly take this story as a fairy tale, it can be understood as an important message of psychic process. Let's look at the story from a psychological point of view.

The author goes into a remote village deep in the forest protected by nature, far removed from the city, with the help of a man who had been there before. One psychological interpretation could be that the Ego, or civilized consciousness, confronts with the depth of our heart, deep with our unconscious (which is remote from our consciousness), with a sacred location, which in Greek, is called a *temenos*. Traveling to such a sacred place with the help of a guide is understood as being guided by Hermes, a psychopomp, a messenger of the heavens, who can go back and forth freely between two worlds (both parts of our psyche).

In the remote village, the author met an old man Mr. M, and was taught a hidden code of Laozi. The *temenos* is the location within, where a wise old man in our psyche lives, and we can confront with wisdom there, which has been kept intact since ancient times. In the village, everything is natural, the people are connected to each other, well balanced, and peaceful, like a Utopia, a world of the great Tao. Deep in our psyches resides such a place: the great Tao. Once you have experienced it, your way of viewing this world is completely different from before.

You see, as you read this book, you might have experienced this process, with your psyche accompanying the author, so you feel inspired and healed, as he was. In a sense, you were led by the auther into the depths of your psyche. But then you have some questions where this village is, and so on, when you come back to reality, the consciousness of this world. Yes, we don't know where the village is, and even if we knew it, we don't think we can live as they do. But once we notice the importance of the way of the human being, the great Tao, there might be something that we can do in this world at this time, in trying to keep the great Tao in our psyche.

There is a famous story in China of the Rain Maker. It goes like this...

A village experienced a severe drought. People tried every way they knew to cause rain, but nothing worked. Finally, they called an old rain maker. He showed up, sniffed the air uncomfortably, and asked the people not to disturb him, and then secluded himself in a hut. Nothing happened for three days. Then, it began to rain, and it even snowed. He explained that the village people were out of order, so the weather was influenced by it. He was also influenced and disturbed in that village, so he tried to recover the state of Tao within himself. It took three days, but the villagers were influenced by him, order in the village was restored, and then it rained as a matter of course.

Transformation within oneself can influence one's world, because the inner and outer are connected deeply, regardless of our being conscious or unconscious of it.

Tao within oneself influences the world outside of ourselves. A condition of Tao, that is, a balanced state of the union of masculinity and femininity, which can be experienced in sexual relationships; numinosity embraced by love, by forces much bigger than ourselves, by the universe and a sense of unity with the universe, called *unus mundus* in alchemy; isn't that the ideal state that people seek? People often seek this ideal state outside of themselves. However, we all have the seed of Tao in the depth of ourselves, not outside. It is far remote and difficult to reach, but paradoxically enough, it is very close to our heart. So you, the readers, might have already felt it in yourself. Feeling yourself being led to that place … that is the value of this book.

Last but not least, I would like to mention the development of this English translation. It was almost ten years ago, when one of my analysands rushed into to our analytical session with the original Japanese version and said, "Please read this book. It is really inspiring!" I wanted to understand what she felt with her acute sensitivity, so I ordered the book and read it. I was very inspired as she was, and wanted some of my former teachers in Switzerland to read it, so I emailed the author to ask if he had a plan to publish it in English in the near future. In fact, I am not the kind of person that ever emails authors, but I felt strongly that this time, I had to. Furthermore, I even felt that the author was waiting for me in a sense. His answer was that he had no plan of an English version at that time, but he also wanted many people to read this book, so he asked me to translate it into English. He even wrote me that he was waiting for a person like me, because he had felt his idea was close to Jungian psychology. I was astonished to read his email, to know he trusted me only from a single email, even without knowing my English ability. I wondered if I could do it, but my hunch said, "Yes," and then my work began. It was not an easy task, honestly speaking, because the contents of this book were transcendent beyond my English ability, but I kept translating page by page, day by day. I was astonished and wondered where my energy came from. Only my wish to let my former teachers read the book, made me keep working.

Finally, I finished translating, asked my private editor to correct my English, and then sent it to my former teachers. My original purpose was accomplished. It was nice that I could do it in time, so that one of them could read it in this world.

Thanks to Murray Stein, my manuscript was sent to Steve Buser and Len Cruz, the publishers at Chiron Publications, and the publishing process began. It took a long time in proceeding forward, because something was missing for this book to be born. I felt something didn't match completely within and without myself. I struggled, not only over publishing this book, but also with my own individuation process. Finally, the right time has come. It was a mysterious moment when I renewed the manuscript under the heaven where the union of masculinity and femininity happened, namely, the solar eclipse, especially on the summer solstice. The seed idea was sowed underground at the right moment. As I was writing this, it even rained and a rainbow connected the earth and the heavens. I sincerely hope that this seed will be fruitful and keep connecting people through trust.

Once again, I would like to express gratitude to a number of people. First of all, to my former teachers in this world and the other, especially Andreas Schweizer, and Ellynor Barz, for their efforts to teach, train and sustain me in becoming an analyst. Without their efforts, the way I am would not have developed. I also thank Murray Stein so much for giving me sound advice and introducing me especially to Chiron Publications. I thank Shen Heyong for writing the preface. It is so precious to me that it is written by him, the specialist on Tao and my Jungian colleague from Laozi's country. It must have been surprising for him to receive my manuscript one day and suddenly be asked to write the forward. But thankfully he accepted my offer willingly, and did the thoughtful work from many perspectives. The message of this book is amplified and deepened thanks to him. Above all, I would like to express my heartfelt gratitude to Steve Buser and Len Cruz, who have accepted my manuscript, and waited for my stepping forward very patiently. I also want to thank Jennifer Fitzgerald, the publisher's editor, who generously supported and guided me. It must have been a tough job to educate a total beginner in book publishing. But thanks to her polite and thoughtful guidance, this book will be born.

And I thank my family, friends, colleagues, analysands, and teachers, and many other people behind the scenes, here, there, and all over the world and universe. Their existence, energies, and ideas continuously support and inspire me.

Above all, I thank the original author Kazuki Chiga, who have shared the meaningful period for this English translation with me. And I also thank my personal editor, Deborah Iwabuchi. She understood the essences that I was going to convey very well, and transformed my English beautifully.

And to the readers: May this book touch the depth of your heart and bear fruit, inside and outside of yourself.

Waiting for the great union within and without.

Kiyomi Hirose
September 2020
Hiroshima, Japan